Anonymous

Scripture Readings

arranged for responsive worship

Anonymous

Scripture Readings
arranged for responsive worship

ISBN/EAN: 9783337285531

Printed in Europe, USA, Canada, Australia, Japan

Cover: Foto ©Lupo / pixelio.de

More available books at **www.hansebooks.com**

ARRANGED FOR

RESPONSIVE WORSHIP

CONTENTS.

	PAGES
THE SANCTUARY AND ITS SERVICE	1– 10
CONFESSION AND PARDON	10– 23
ADORATION AND THANKSGIVING	23– 32
THE MAJESTY AND HOLINESS OF GOD	33– 39
GOD'S GLORY IN NATURE	39– 49
GOD'S GLORY IN PROVIDENCE AND GRACE	50– 61
HUMAN FRAILTY	62– 67
MAN'S REFUGE IN GOD	67– 88
GOD OUR DEFENDER AND JUDGE	89– 99
THE WAY OF WISDOM	99–108
THE MESSIAH AND HIS KINGDOM	109–142

THE TEN COMMANDMENTS.

And God spake all these words, saying,

I. I am the Lord thy God, which have brought thee out of the land of Egypt, out of the house of bondage. Thou shalt have no other gods before me.

II. Thou shalt not make unto thee any graven image, or any likeness of any thing that is in heaven above, or that is in the earth beneath, or that is in the water under the earth: thou shalt not bow down thyself to them, nor serve them: for I the Lord thy God am a jealous God, visiting the iniquity of the fathers upon the children, unto the third and fourth generation of them that hate me, and showing mercy unto thousands of them that love me, and keep my commandments.

III. Thou shalt not take the name of the Lord thy God in vain; for the Lord will not hold him guiltless that taketh his name in vain.

IV. Remember the sabbath day, to keep it holy. Six days shalt thou labor, and do all thy work: but the seventh day is the sabbath of the Lord thy God: in it thou shalt not do any work, thou, nor thy son, nor thy daughter, thy manservant, nor thy maidservant, nor thy cattle, nor thy stranger that is within thy gates: for in six days the Lord made heaven and earth, the sea, and all that in them is, and rested the seventh day: wherefore the Lord blessed the sabbath day, and hallowed it.

V. Honor thy father and thy mother: that thy days may be long upon the land which the Lord thy God giveth thee.

VI. Thou shalt not kill.

VII. Thou shalt not commit adultery.

VIII. Thou shalt not steal.

IX. Thou shalt not bear false witness against thy neighbor.

X. Thou shalt not covet thy neighbor's house, thou shalt not covet thy neighbor's wife, nor his manservant, nor his maidservant, nor his ox, nor his ass, nor any thing that is thy neighbor's.

REMEMBER the words of the Lord Jesus, how he said: The first of all the commandments is, Hear, O Israel; The Lord our God is one Lord:

And thou shalt love the Lord thy God with all thy heart, and with all thy soul, and with all thy mind, and with all thy strength.

This is the first commandment. And the second is like, namely this:

Thou shalt love thy neighbor as thyself.

On these two commandments hang all the Law and the Prophets.

THE SANCTUARY AND ITS SERVICE.

FIRST LESSON.

Ps. 1. BLESSED is the man that walketh not in the counsel of the wicked,
Nor standeth in the way of the sinners, nor sitteth in the seat of the scornful.
But his delight is in the law of the Lord;
And in his law doth he meditate day and night.
And he shall be like a tree planted by the streams of water,
That bringeth forth its fruit in its season,
Whose leaf also doth not wither;
And whatsoever he doeth shall prosper.
The wicked are not so; but are like the chaff which the wind driveth away.
Therefore the wicked shall not stand in the judgment, nor sinners in the congregation of the righteous.
For the Lord knoweth the way of the righteous:
But the way of the wicked shall perish.

Ps. 15. LORD, who shall sojourn in thy tabernacle? who shall dwell in thy holy hill?
He that walketh uprightly and worketh righteousness, and speaketh truth in his heart.
He that slandereth not with his tongue, nor doeth evil to his friend,
Nor taketh up a reproach against his neighbor.
In whose eyes a reprobate is despised;
But he honoreth them that fear the Lord.
He that sweareth to his own hurt, and changeth **not,**
He that putteth not out his money to usury,
Nor taketh reward against the innocent.
He that doeth these things shall never be moved.

(1)

Ps. 112. Praise ye the Lord. Blessed is the man that feareth the Lord,
That delighteth greatly in his commandments.

His seed shall be mighty upon earth:
The generation of the upright shall be blessed.

Wealth and riches are in his house:
And his righteousness endureth for ever.

Unto the upright there ariseth light in the darkness:
He is gracious, and full of compassion, and righteous.

Well is it with the man that dealeth graciously and lendeth;
He shall maintain his cause in judgment.

or he shall never be moved:
The righteous shall be had in everlasting remembrance.

He shall not be afraid of evil tidings:
His heart is fixed, trusting in the Lord.

His heart is established, he shall not be afraid,
Until he see his desire upon his adversaries.

He hath dispersed, he hath given to the needy; his righteousness endureth for ever:
His horn shall be exalted with honor.

Ps. 131. Lord, my heart is not haughty, nor mine eyes lofty;
Neither do I exercise myself in great matters, or in things too wonderful for me.

Surely I have stilled and quieted my soul;
Like a weaned child with his mother,

My soul is with me like a weaned child.
O Israel, hope in the Lord from this time forth and for evermore.

SECOND LESSON.

Ps. 101. I will sing of mercy and judgment:
Unto thee, O Lord, will I sing praises.

I will behave myself wisely in a perfect way:
O when wilt thou come unto me?

I will walk within my house with a perfect heart.
I will set no base thing before mine eyes:

I hate the work of them that turn aside; it shall not cleave unto me.
A froward heart shall depart from me: I will know no evil thing.

Whoso privily slandereth his neighbor, him will I destroy:
Him that hath an high look and a proud heart will I not suffer.

Mine eyes shall be upon the faithful of the land, that they may dwell with me:
He that walketh in a perfect way, he shall minister unto me.

He that worketh deceit shall not dwell within my house:
He that speaketh falsehood shall not be established before mine eyes.

Morning by morning will I destroy all the wicked of the land;
To cut off all the workers of iniquity from the city of the Lord.

Ps. 132. LORD, remember for David all his affliction;
How he sware unto the Lord, and vowed unto the Mighty One of Jacob:

Surely I will not come into the tabernacle of my house, nor go up into my bed;
I will not give sleep to mine eyes, or slumber to mine eyelids;

Until I find out a place for the Lord, a tabernacle for the Mighty One of Jacob.
Lo, we heard of it in Ephrathah: we found it in the field of the wood.

We will go into his tabernacles:
We will worship at his footstool.

Arise, O Lord, into thy resting place;
Thou, and the ark of thy strength.

Let thy priests be clothed with righteousness;
And let thy saints shout for joy.

For thy servant David's sake turn not away the face of thine anointed.
The Lord hath sworn unto David in truth;

He will not turn from it:
Of the fruit of thy body will I set upon thy throne.

If thy children will keep my covenant and my testimony that I shall teach them,
Their children also shall sit upon thy throne for evermore.

For the Lord hath chosen Zion;
He hath desired it for his habitation.

This is my resting place for ever:
Here will I dwell; for I have desired it.

I will abundantly bless her provision:
I will satisfy her poor with bread.

Her priests also will I clothe with salvation:
And her saints shall shout aloud for joy.

There will I make the horn of David to bud:
I have ordained a lamp for mine anointed.

His enemies will I clothe with shame:
But upon himself shall his crown flourish.

THIRD LESSON.

Ps. 48. Great is the Lord, and highly to be praised,
In the city of our God, in his holy mountain.

Beautiful in elevation, the joy of the whole earth, is mount Zion, *on* the sides of the north,
The city of the great King.

God hath made himself known in her palaces for a refuge.
For, lo, the kings assembled themselves, they passed by together.

They saw it, then they were amazed;
They were dismayed, they hasted away.

Trembling took hold of them there; pain, as of a woman in travail.
With the east wind thou breakest the ships of Tarshish.

As we have heard, so have we seen in the city of the Lord of hosts, in the city of our God:
God will establish it for ever.

We have thought on thy loving kindness, O God, in the midst of thy temple.
As is thy name, O God, so is thy praise unto the ends of the earth:

Thy right hand is full of righteousness.
Let mount Zion be glad,

Let the daughters of Judah rejoice,
Because of thy judgments.

Walk about Zion, and go round about her:
Tell the towers thereof.

Mark ye well her bulwarks, consider her palaces;
That ye may tell it to the generation following.

For this God is our God for ever and ever:
He will be our guide even unto death.

Ps. 63. O GOD, thou art my God; earnestly will I seek thee:
My soul thirsteth for thee, my flesh longeth for thee,

In a dry and weary land, where no water is.
So have I looked upon thee in the sanctuary, to see thy power and thy glory.

For thy loving kindness is better than life;
My lips shall praise thee.

So will I bless thee while I live:
I will lift up my hands in thy name.

My soul shall be satisfied as with marrow and fatness;
And my mouth shall praise thee with joyful lips;

When I remember thee upon my bed,
And meditate on thee in the night watches.

For thou hast been my help,
And in the shadow of thy wings will I rejoice.

My soul followeth hard after thee:
Thy right hand upholdeth me.

But those that seek my soul, to destroy it, shall go into the lower parts of the earth.
They shall be given over to the power of the sword:

They shall be a portion for foxes.
But the king shall rejoice in God;

Every one that sweareth by him shall glory;
For the mouth of them that speak lies shall be stopped.

Ps. 95. O COME, let us sing unto the Lord:
Let us make a joyful noise to the rock of our salvation.

Let us come before his presence with thanksgiving,
Let us make a joyful noise unto him with psalms.

For the Lord is a great God, and a great King above all gods.
In his hand are the deep places of the earth;

The heights of the mountains are his also.
The sea is his, and he made it; and his hands formed the dry land.

O come, let us worship and bow down;
Let us kneel before the Lord our Maker:

For he is our God,
And we are the people of his pasture, and the sheep of his hand.

FOURTH LESSON.

Ps. 84. How amiable are thy tabernacles, O Lord of hosts!
My soul longeth, yea, even fainteth for the courts of the Lord;
My heart and my flesh cry out unto the living God.
Yea, the sparrow hath found her an house, and the swallow a nest for herself, where she may lay her young,
Even thine altars, O Lord of hosts,
My King, and my God.
Blessed are they that dwell in thy house:
They will be still praising thee.
Blessed is the man whose strength is in thee;
In whose heart are the high ways to Zion.
Passing through the valley of Weeping they make it a place of springs;
Yea, the early rain covereth it with blessings.
They go from strength to strength,
Every one of them appeareth before God in Zion.
O Lord God of hosts, hear my prayer:
Give ear, O God of Jacob.
Behold, O God our shield, and look upon the face of thine anointed.
For a day in thy courts is better than a thousand.
I had rather be a doorkeeper in the house of my God,
Than to dwell in the tents of wickedness.
For the Lord God is a sun and a shield:
The Lord will give grace and glory:
No good thing will he withhold from them that walk uprightly.
O Lord of hosts, blessed is the man that trusteth in thee.

Ps. 100. Make a joyful noise unto the Lord, all ye lands.
Serve the Lord with gladness; come before his presence with singing.
Know ye that the Lord he is God:
It is he that hath made us, and we are his; we are his people, and the sheep of his pasture.
Enter into his gates with thanksgiving, and into his courts with praise:
Give thanks unto him, and bless his name.
For the Lord is good; his mercy *endureth* for ever;
And his faithfulness unto all generations.

Ps. 122.   I WAS glad when they said unto me, let us go unto the house of the Lord.
  Our feet are standing within thy gates, O Jerusalem;
Jerusalem, that art builded as a city that is compact together:
  Whither the tribes go up, even the tribes of the Lord,
An ordinance for Israel.
  To give thanks unto the name of the Lord.
For there are set thrones for judgment,
  The thrones of the house of David.
Pray for the peace of Jerusalem:
  They shall prosper that love thee.
Peace be within thy walls,
  And prosperity within thy palaces.
For my brethren and companions' sakes, I will now say, Peace be within thee.
  For the sake of the house of the Lord our God I will seek thy good.

FIFTH LESSON.

Ps. 66.   MAKE a joyful noise unto God, all the earth:
  Sing forth the glory of his name: make his praise glorious.
Say unto God, How terrible are thy works!
  Through the greatness of thy power shall thine enemies submit themselves unto thee.
All the earth shall worship thee, and shall sing unto thee;
  They shall sing to thy name.
Come, and see the works of God;
  He is terrible in his doing toward the children of men.
He turned the sea into dry land:
  They went through the river on foot:
There did we rejoice in him.
  He ruleth by his might for ever;
His eyes observe the nations:
  Let not the rebellious exalt themselves.
O bless our God, ye peoples, and make the voice of his praise to be heard:
  Which holdeth our soul in life, and suffereth not our feet to be moved.
For thou, O God, hast proved us: thou hast tried us, as silver is tried.
  Thou broughtest us into the net;

Thou layedst a sore burden upon our loins.
  Thou hast caused men to ride over our heads;
We went through fire and through water;
  But thou broughtest us out into a wealthy place.
I will come into thy house with burnt offerings, I will pay thee my vows,
  Which my lips have uttered, and my mouth hath spoken, when I was in distress.
I will offer unto thee burnt offerings of fatlings, with the incense of rams;
  I will offer bullocks with goats.
Come, and hear, all ye that fear God,
  And I will declare what he hath done for my soul.
I cried unto him with my mouth, and he was extolled with my tongue.
  If I regard iniquity in my heart, the Lord will not hear;
But verily God hath heard; he hath attended to the voice of my prayer.
  Blessed be God, which hath not turned away my prayer, nor his mercy from me.

Ps. 87. HIS foundation is in the holy mountains.
  The Lord loveth the gates of Zion more than all the dwellings of Jacob.
Glorious things are spoken of thee, O city of God.
  I will make mention of Rahab and Babylon as among them that know me:
Behold Philistia, and Tyre, with Ethiopia;
  This one was born there.
Yea, of Zion it shall be said, This one and that one was born in her;
  And the Most High himself shall establish her.
The Lord shall count, when he writeth up the peoples, this one was born there.
  They that sing as well as they that dance shall say, All my fountains are in thee.

Ps. 134. BEHOLD, bless ye the Lord, all ye servants of the Lord,
  Which by night stand in the house of the Lord.
Lift up your hands to the sanctuary,
  And bless ye the Lord.
The Lord bless thee out of Zion;
  Even he that made heaven and earth.

SIXTH LESSON.

Ps. 42. As the hart panteth after the water brooks, so panteth my soul after thee, O God.
  My soul thirsteth for God, for the living God: when shall I come and appear before God?
  My tears have been my meat day and night, while they continually say unto me, Where is thy God?
  These things I remember, and pour out my soul within me,
  How I went with the throng, and led them to the house of God,
  With the voice of joy and praise, a multitude keeping holyday.
  Why art thou cast down, O my soul?
  And why art thou disquieted within me?
  Hope thou in God: for I shall yet praise him
  For the help of his countenance.
  O my God, my soul is cast down within me:
  Therefore do I remember thee from the land of Jordan, and the Hermons, from the hill Mizar.
  Deep calleth unto deep at the noise of thy water-spouts:
  All thy waves and thy billows are gone over me.
  Yet the Lord will command his loving kindness in the day-time,
  And in the night his song shall be with me, even a prayer unto the God of my life.
  I will say unto God my rock, Why hast thou forgotten me?
  Why go I mourning because of the oppression of the enemy?
  As with a sword in my bones, mine adversaries reproach me;
  While they continually say unto me, Where is thy God?
  Why art thou cast down, O my soul?
  And why art thou disquieted within me?
  Hope thou in God: for I shall yet praise him,
  Who is the help of my countenance, and my God.

Ps. 43. JUDGE me, O God, and plead my cause against an ungodly nation:
  O deliver me from the deceitful and unjust man.
  For thou art the God of my strength: why hast thou cast me off?
  Why go I mourning because of the oppression of the enemy?
  O send out thy light and thy truth; let them lead me:
  Let them bring me unto thy holy hill, and to thy tabernacles.

Then will I go unto the altar of God, unto God my exceeding joy:
And upon the harp will I praise thee, O God, my God.
Why art thou cast down, O my soul?
And why art thou disquieted within me?
Hope thou in God: for I shall yet praise him,
Who is the help of my countenance, and my God.

SEVENTH LESSON.

Ps. 51. HAVE mercy upon me, O God, according to thy loving kindness
According to the multitude of thy tender mercies blot out my transgressions.
Wash me thoroughly from mine iniquity,
And cleanse me from my sin.
For I acknowledge my transgressions:
And my sin is ever before me.
Against thee, thee only, have I sinned,
And done that which is evil in thy sight:
That thou mayest be justified when thou speakest,
And be clear when thou judgest.
Behold, I was shapen in iniquity;
And in sin did my mother conceive me.
Behold, thou desirest truth in the inward parts:
And in the hidden part thou shalt make me to know wisdom.
Purge me with hyssop, and I shall be clean:
Wash me, and I shall be whiter than snow.
Make me to hear joy and gladness;
That the bones which thou hast broken may rejoice.
Hide thy face from my sins,
And blot out all mine iniquities.
Create in me a clean heart, O God;
And renew a right spirit within me.
Cast me not away from thy presence;
And take not thy Holy Spirit from me.
Restore unto me the joy of thy salvation:
And uphold me with a willing spirit.

Then will I teach transgressors thy ways;
And sinners shall be converted unto thee.

Deliver me from bloodguiltiness, O God, thou God of my salvation;
And my tongue shall sing aloud of thy righteousness.

O Lord, open thou my lips;
And my mouth shall shew forth thy praise.

For thou delightest not in sacrifice; else would I give it:
Thou hast no pleasure in burnt offering.

The sacrifices of God are a broken spirit:
A broken and a contrite heart, O God, thou wilt not despise.

Do good in thy good pleasure unto Zion:
Build thou the walls of Jerusalem.

Then shalt thou delight in the sacrifices of righteousness, in burnt offering and whole burnt offering:
Then shall they offer bullocks upon thine altar.

Ps. 130. OUT of the depths have I cried unto thee, O Lord. Lord, hear my voice:
Let thine ears be attentive to the voice of my supplications.

If thou, Lord, shouldest mark iniquities,
O Lord, who shall stand?

But there is forgiveness with thee,
That thou mayest be feared.

I wait for the Lord, my soul doth wait,
And in his word do I hope.

My soul waiteth for the Lord more than watchmen *wait* for the morning;
Yea, more than watchmen for the morning.

O Israel, hope in the Lord; for with the Lord there is mercy, and with him is plenteous redemption.
And he shall redeem Israel from all his iniquities.

CONFESSION AND PARDON.

EIGHTH LESSON.

Ps. 25. UNTO thee, O Lord, do I lift up my soul.
O my God, in thee have I trusted,
Let me not be ashamed;
Let not mine enemies triumph over me.
Yea, none that wait on thee shall be ashamed:
They shall be ashamed that deal treacherously without cause.
Shew me thy ways, O Lord; teach me thy paths.
Guide me in thy truth, and teach me;
For thou art the God of my salvation;
On thee do I wait all the day.
Remember, O Lord, thy tender mercies and thy loving kindnesses:
For they have been ever of old.
Remember not the sins of my youth, nor my transgressions:
According to thy loving kindness remember thou me, for thy goodness' sake, O Lord.
Good and upright is the Lord:
Therefore will he instruct sinners in the way.
The meek will he guide in judgment:
And the meek will he teach his way.
All the paths of the Lord are loving kindness and truth
Unto such as keep his covenant and his testimonies.
For thy name's sake, O Lord,
Pardon mine iniquity, for it is great.
What man is he that feareth the Lord?
Him shall he instruct in the way that he shall choose.
His soul shall dwell at ease;
And his seed shall inherit the land.
The secret of the Lord is with them that fear him,
And he will shew them his covenant.
Mine eyes are ever toward the Lord;
For he shall pluck my feet out of the net.
Turn thee unto me, and have mercy upon me;
For I am desolate and afflicted.
The troubles of my heart are enlarged:
O bring thou me out of my distresses.

Consider mine affliction and my travail;
   And forgive all my sins.

Consider mine enemies, for they are many;
   And they hate me with cruel hatred.

O keep my soul, and deliver me:
   Let me not be ashamed, for I put my trust in thee.

Let integrity and uprightness preserve me; for I wait on thee.
   Redeem Israel, O God, out of all his troubles.

Ps. 85. LORD, thou hast been favorable unto thy land:
   Thou hast brought back the captivity of Jacob.

Thou hast forgiven the iniquity of thy people;
   Thou hast covered all their sin.

Thou hast taken away all thy wrath:
   Thou hast turned thyself from the fierceness of thine anger.

Turn us, O God of our salvation,
   And cause thine indignation toward us to cease.

Wilt thou be angry with us for ever?
   Wilt thou draw out thine anger to all generations?

Wilt thou not quicken us again:
   That thy people may rejoice in thee?

Shew us thy mercy, O Lord,
   And grant us thy salvation.

I will hear what God the Lord will speak: for he will speak peace unto his people, and to his saints:
   But let them not turn again to folly.

Surely his salvation is nigh them that fear him;
   That glory may dwell in our land.

Mercy and truth are met together;
   Righteousness and peace have kissed each other.

Truth springeth out of the earth;
   And righteousness hath looked down from heaven.

Yea, the Lord shall give that which is good;
   And our land shall yield her increase.

Righteousness shall go before him;
   And shall make his footsteps a way to walk in.

CONFESSION AND PARDON.

NINTH LESSON.

Ps. 36. THE transgression of the wicked saith within my heart,
There is no fear of God before his eyes.

For he flattereth himself in his own eyes,
That his iniquity shall not be found out and be hated.

The words of his mouth are iniquity and deceit:
He hath left off to be wise and to do good.

He deviseth iniquity upon his bed;
He setteth himself in a way that is not good; he abhorreth not evil.

Thy loving kindness, O Lord, is in the heavens;
Thy faithfulness reacheth unto the skies.

Thy righteousness is like the mountains of God; thy judgments are a great deep:
O Lord, thou preserveth man and beast.

How precious is thy loving kindness, O God!
And the children of men take refuge under the shadow of thy wings.

They shall be abundantly satisfied with the fatness of thy house;
And thou shalt make them drink of the river of thy pleasures.

For with thee is the fountain of life:
In thy light shall we see light.

O continue thy loving kindness unto them that know thee;
And thy righteousness to the upright in heart.

Let not the foot of pride come against me,
And let not the hand of the wicked drive me away.

There are the workers of iniquity fallen:
They are thrust down, and shall not be able to rise.

Ps. 80. GIVE ear, O Shepherd of Israel, thou that leadest Joseph like a flock;
Thou that sittest upon the cherubim, shine forth.

Before Ephraim and Benjamin and Manasseh, stir up thy might,
And come to save us.

Turn us again, O God;
And cause thy face to shine, and we shall be saved.

O Lord God of hosts,
How long wilt thou be angry against the prayer of thy people?

Thou hast fed them with the bread of tears,
  And given them tears to drink in large measure.
Thou makest us a strife unto our neighbors:
  And our enemies laugh among themselves.
Turn us again, O God of hosts;
  And cause thy face to shine, and we shall be saved.
Thou broughtest a vine out of Egypt:
  Thou didst drive out the nations, and plantedst it.
Thou preparedst *room* before it,
  And it took deep root, and filled the land.
The mountains were covered with the shadow of it,
  And the boughs thereof were like cedars of God.
She sent out her branches unto the sea,
  And her shoots unto the River.
Why hast thou broken down her fences,
  So that all they which pass by the way do pluck her?
The boar out of the wood doth ravage it,
  And the wild beasts of the field feed on it.
Turn again, we beseech thee, O God of hosts:
  Look down from heaven, and behold, and visit this vine,
And the stock which thy right hand hath planted,
  And the branch that thou madest strong for thyself.
It is burned with fire, it is cut down:
  They perish at the rebuke of thy countenance.
Let thy hand be upon the man of thy right hand,
  Upon the son of man whom thou madest strong for thyself.
So shall we not go back from thee:
  Quicken thou us, and we will call upon thy name.
Turn us again, O Lord God of hosts;
  Cause thy face to shine, and we shall be saved.

CONFESSION AND PARDON.

TENTH LESSON.

Ps. 6.   O Lord, rebuke me not in thine anger,
  Neither chasten me in thy hot displeasure.
Have mercy upon me, O Lord; for I am withered away:
  O Lord, heal me; for my bones are vexed.
My soul also is sore vexed:
  And thou, O Lord, how long?
Return, O Lord, deliver my soul:
  Save me for thy loving kindness' sake.
For in death there is no remembrance of thee:
  In Sheol who shall give thee thanks?
I am weary with my groaning; every night make I my bed to swim;
  I water my couch with my tears.
Mine eye wasteth away because of grief;
  It waxeth old because of all mine adversaries.
Depart from me, all ye workers of iniquity;
  For the Lord hath heard the voice of my weeping.
The Lord hath heard my supplication;
  The Lord will receive my prayer.
All mine enemies shall be ashamed and sore vexed:
  They shall turn back, they shall be ashamed suddenly.

Ps. 32.   Blessed is he whose transgression is forgiven, whose sin is covered.
  Blessed is the man unto whom the Lord imputeth not iniquity,
And in whose spirit there is no guile.
  When I kept silence, my bones waxed old through my roaring all the day long.
For day and night thy hand was heavy upon me:
  My moisture was changed as with the drought of summer.
I acknowledged my sin unto thee, and mine iniquity have I not hid:
  I said, I will confess my transgressions unto the Lord; and thou forgavest the iniquity of my sin.
For this let every one that is godly pray unto thee in a time when thou mayest be found:
  Surely when the great waters overflow they shall not reach unto him.
Thou art my hiding place; thou wilt preserve me from trouble;
  Thou wilt compass me about with songs of deliverance.

CONFESSION AND PARDON.

I will instruct thee and teach thee in the way which thou shalt go:
I will counsel thee with mine eye upon thee.

Be ye not as the horse, or as the mule, which have no understanding:
Whose trappings must be bit and bridle to hold them in, else they will not come near unto thee.

Many sorrows shall be to the wicked:
But he that trusteth in the Lord, mercy shall compass him about.

Be glad in the Lord, and rejoice, ye righteous:
And shout for joy, all ye that are upright in heart.

ELEVENTH LESSON.

Ps. 40. I WAITED patiently for the Lord;
And he inclined unto me, and heard my cry.

He brought me up also out of an horrible pit, out of the miry clay:
And he set my feet upon a rock, and established my goings.

And he hath put a new song in my mouth, even praise unto our God:
Many shall see it, and fear, and shall trust in the Lord.

Blessed is the man that maketh the Lord his trust,
And respecteth not the proud, nor such as turn aside to lies.

Many, O Lord my God, are the wonderful works which thou hast done,
And thy thoughts which are to us-ward:

They cannot be set in order unto thee;
If I would declare and speak of them, they are more than can be numbered.

Sacrifice and offering thou hast no delight in; mine ears hast thou opened:
Burnt offering and sin offering hast thou not required.

Then said I, Lo, I am come;
In the roll of the book it is written of me:

I delight to do thy will, O my God;
Yea, thy law is within my heart.

I have published righteousness in the great congregation:
Lo, I will not refrain my lips, O Lord, thou knowest.

I have not hid thy righteousness within my heart: I have declared thy faithfulness and thy salvation:
I have not concealed thy loving-kindness and thy truth from the great congregation.

CONFESSION AND PARDON.

Withhold not thou thy tender mercies from me, O Lord:
Let thy loving kindness and thy truth continually preserve me.

For innumerable evils have compassed me about, mine iniquities have overtaken me, so that I am not able to look up;
They are more than the hairs of mine head, and my heart hath failed me.

Be pleased, O Lord, to deliver me:
Make haste to help me, O Lord.

Let them be ashamed and confounded together that seek after my soul to destroy it:
Let them be turned backward and brought to dishonor that delight in my hurt.

Let them be desolate by reason of their shame that say unto me, Aha, Aha.
Let all those that seek thee rejoice and be glad in thee:

Let such as love thy salvation say continually,
The Lord be magnified.

But I am poor and needy;
Yet the Lord thinketh upon me:

Thou art my help and my deliverer;
Make no tarrying, O my God.

JOB 33. FOR God speaketh once,
Yea twice, though man regardeth it not.

In a dream, in a vision of the night, when deep sleep falleth upon men,
In slumberings upon the bed;

Then he openeth the ears of men, and sealeth their instruction,
That he may withdraw man from his purpose, and hide pride from man;

He keepeth back his soul from the pit,
And his life from perishing by the sword.

If there be with him an angel, an interpreter, one among a thousand,
To shew unto man what is right for him;

Then he is gracious unto him, and saith,
Deliver him from going down to the pit, I have found a ransom.

His flesh shall be fresher than a child's; he returneth to the days of his youth:
He prayeth unto God, and he is favorable unto him;

So that he seeth his face with joy:
And he restoreth unto man his righteousness.

TWELFTH LESSON.

DEUT. 28. AND it shall come to pass, if thou shalt hearken diligently unto the voice of the Lord thy God,
To observe to do all his commandments which I command thee this day,
That the Lord thy God will set thee on high above all the nations of the earth:
And all these blessings shall come upon thee, and overtake thee, if thou shalt hearken unto the voice of the Lord thy God.
Blessed shalt thou be in the city,
And blessed shalt thou be in the field.
Blessed shall be the fruit of thy body, and the fruit of thy ground, and the fruit of thy cattle,
The increase of thy kine, and the young of thy flock.
Blessed shall be thy basket and thy kneadingtrough.
Blessed shalt thou be when thou comest in, and blessed shalt thou be when thou goest out.
The Lord shall cause thine enemies that rise up against thee to be smitten before thee:
They shall come out against thee one way, and shall flee before thee seven ways.
The Lord shall command the blessing upon thee in thy barns, and in all that thou puttest thine hand unto;
And he shall bless thee in the land which the Lord thy God giveth thee.
The Lord shall establish thee for an holy people unto himself, as he hath sworn unto thee;
If thou shalt keep the commandments of the Lord thy God, and walk in his ways.
And all the peoples of the earth shall see that thou art called by the name of the Lord;
And they shall be afraid of thee.
And the Lord shall make thee plenteous for good, in the fruit of thy body, and in the fruit of thy cattle, and in the fruit of thy ground,
In the land which the Lord sware unto thy fathers to give thee.
The Lord shall open unto thee his good treasure the heaven to give the rain of thy land in its season, and to bless all the work of thine hand:
And thou shalt lend unto many nations, and thou shalt not borrow.
And the Lord shalt make thee the head, and not the tail;
And thou shalt be above only, and thou shalt not be beneath;

CONFESSION AND PARDON.

If thou shalt hearken unto the commandments of the Lord thy God, which I command thee this day, to observe and to do *them;*
And shalt not turn aside from any of the words which I command you this day, to the right hand, or to the left, to go after other gods to serve them.

HOSEA 14. O ISRAEL, return unto the Lord thy God;
For thou hast fallen by thine iniquity.

Take with you words, and return unto the Lord: say unto him, Take away all iniquity, and accept that which is good:
So shall we render as bullocks the offering of our lips.

Asshur shall not save us;
We will not ride upon horses:

Neither will we say any more to the work of our hands, *Ye are* our gods:
For in thee the fatherless findeth mercy.

I will heal their backsliding, I will love them freely:
For mine anger is turned away from him.

I will be as the dew unto Israel:
He shall blossom as the lily, and cast forth his roots as Lebanon.

His branches shall spread,
And his beauty shall be as the olive tree, and his smell as Lebanon.

They that dwell under his shadow shall return; they shall revive *as* the corn, and blossom as the vine:
The scent thereof shall be as the wine of Lebanon.

Ephraim *shall say,* What have I to do any more with idols?
I have answered, and will regard him: I am like a green fir tree; from me is thy fruit found.

Who is wise, and he shall understand these things? prudent, and he shall know them?
For the ways of the Lord are right, and the just shall walk in them; but transgressors shall fall therein.

THIRTEENTH LESSON.

JOEL 2. Blow ye the trumpet in Zion, and sound an alarm in my holy mountain; let all the inhabitants of the land tremble:
For the day of the Lord cometh, for it is nigh at hand;
A day of darkness and gloominess, a day of clouds and thick darkness, as the dawn spread upon the mountains:
For the day of the Lord is great and very terrible; and who can abide it?
Yet even now, saith the Lord, turn ye unto me with all your heart, and with fasting, and with weeping, and with mourning:
And rend your heart, and not your garments, and turn unto the Lord your God;
For he is gracious and full of compassion,
Slow to anger, and plenteous in mercy, and repenteth him of the evil.
Who knoweth whether he will not turn and repent, and leave a blessing behind him,
Even a meal offering and a drink offering unto the Lord your God?
Blow the trumpet in Zion,
Sanctify a fast, call a solemn assembly:
Gather the people, sanctify the congregation, assemble the old men, gather the children, and those that suck the breasts:
Let the bridegroom go forth of his chamber, and the bride out of her closet.
Let the priests, the ministers of the Lord, weep between the porch and the altar,
And let them say, spare thy people, O Lord,
And give not thine heritage to reproach, that the nations should rule over them:
Wherefore should they say among the peoples, Where is their God?
Then was the Lord jealous for his land,
And had pity on his people.
Fear not, O land, be glad and rejoice;
For the Lord hath done great things.
Be not afraid, ye beasts of the field; for the pastures of the wilderness do spring,
For the tree beareth her fruit, the fig tree and the vine do yield their strength.
Be glad then, ye children of Zion,
And rejoice in the Lord your God:

ADORATION AND THANKSGIVING.

For he giveth you the former rain in just measure, and he causeth to come down for you the rain,
The former rain and the latter rain, in the first month.

And the floors shall be full of wheat,
And the fats shall overflow with wine and oil.

And ye shall eat in plenty and be satisfied, and shall praise the name of the Lord your God, that hath dealt wondrously with you:
And my people shall never be ashamed.

And ye shall know that I am in the midst of Israel, and that I am the Lord your God, and there is none else:
And my people shall never be ashamed.

And it shall come to pass afterward, that I will pour out my spirit upon all flesh;
And your sons and your daughters shall prophesy,

Your old men shall dream dreams,
Your young men shall see visions:

And also upon the servants and upon the handmaids in those days will I pour out my spirit.
And I will shew wonders in the heavens and in the earth, blood, and fire, and pillars of smoke.

The sun shall be turned into darkness, and the moon into blood,
Before the great and terrible day of the Lord come.

And it shall come to pass, that whosoever shall call on the name of the Lord shall be delivered:
For in mount Zion and in Jerusalem there shall be those that escape, as the Lord hath said, and among the remnant those whom the Lord doth call.

FOURTEENTH LESSON.

Ps. 92. It is a good thing to give thanks unto the Lord,
And to sing praises unto thy name, O Most High:

To shew forth thy loving kindness in the morning,
And thy faithfulness every night,

With an instrument of ten strings, and with the psaltery;
With a solemn sound upon the harp:

For thou, Lord, hast made me glad through thy work:
   I will triumph in the works of thy hands.
How great are thy works, O Lord!
   Thy thoughts are very deep.
A brutish man knoweth not;
   Neither doth a fool understand this:
When the wicked spring as the grass,
   And when all the workers of iniquity do flourish;
It is that they shall be destroyed for ever:
   But thou, O Lord, art on high for evermore.
For, lo, thine enemies, O Lord, for, lo, thine enemies shall perish;
   All the workers of iniquity shall be scattered.
But my horn hast thou exalted like *the horn of* the wild-ox:
   I am anointed with fresh oil.
Mine eye also hath seen *my desire* on mine enemies,
   Mine ears have heard my desire of the evil-doers that rise up against me.
The righteous shall flourish like the palm tree:
   He shall grow like a cedar in Lebanon.
They are planted in the house of the Lord,
   They shall flourish in the courts of our God.
They shall still bring forth fruit in old age;
   They shall be full of sap and green:
To shew that the Lord is upright;
   He is my rock, and there is no unrighteousness in him.

Ps. 138. I WILL give thee thanks with my whole heart:
   Before the gods will I sing praises unto thee.
I will worship toward thy holy temple,
   And give thanks unto thy name for thy loving kindness and for thy truth:
For thou hast magnified thy word above all thy name.
   In the day that I called thou answeredst me, thou diast encourage me with strength in my soul.
All the kings of the earth shall give thee thanks, O Lord,
   For they have heard the words of thy mouth.
Yea, they shall sing of the ways of the Lord;
   For great is the glory of the Lord.

ADORATION AND THANKSGIVING.

For though the Lord be high, yet hath he respect unto the lowly :
But the haughty he knoweth from afar.

Though I walk in the midst of trouble, thou wilt revive me ;
Thou shalt stretch forth thine hand against the wrath of mine enemies,

And thy right hand shall save me.
The Lord will perfect that which concerneth me :

Thy mercy, O Lord, *endureth* for ever ;
Forsake not the works of thine own hands.

FIFTEENTH LESSON.

Ps. 103. BLESS the Lord, O my soul ;
And all that is within me, bless his holy name.

Bless the Lord, O my soul,
And forget not all his benefits :

Who forgiveth all thine iniquities ;
Who healeth all thy diseases ;

Who redeemeth thy life from destruction ;
Who crowneth thee with loving kindness and tender mercies :

Who satisfieth thy desire with good things ;
So that thy youth is renewed like the eagle.

The Lord executeth righteous acts,
And judgments for all that are oppressed.

He made known his ways unto Moses,
His doings unto the children of Israel.

The Lord is full of compassion and gracious,
Slow to anger, and plenteous in mercy.

He will not always chide ;
Neither will he keep his anger for ever.

He hath not dealt with us after our sins,
Nor rewarded us after our iniquities.

For as the heaven is high above the earth,
So great is his mercy toward them that fear him.

As far as the east is from the west,
So far hath he removed our transgressions from us.

ADORATION AND THANKSGIVING.

Like as a father pitieth his children,
So the Lord pitieth them that fear him.

For he knoweth our frame;
He remembereth that we are dust.

As for man, his days are as grass;
As a flower of the field, so he flourisheth.

For the wind passeth over it, and it is gone;
And the place thereof shall know it no more.

But the mercy of the Lord is from everlasting to everlasting upon them that fear him,
And his righteousness unto children's children;

To such as keep his covenant,
And to those that remember his precepts to do them.

The Lord hath established his throne in the heavens;
And his kingdom ruleth over all.

Bless the Lord, ye angels of his:
Ye mighty in strength, that fulfill his word, hearkening unto the voice of his word.

Bless the Lord, all ye his hosts;
Ye ministers of his, that do his pleasure.

Bless the Lord, all ye his works, in all places of his dominion:
Bless the Lord, O my soul.

Ps. 108. My heart is fixed, O God;
I will sing, yea, I will sing praises, even with my glory.

Awake, psaltery and harp:
I myself will awake right early.

I will give thanks unto thee, O Lord, among the peoples:
And I will sing praises unto thee among the nations.

For thy mercy is great above the heavens,
And thy truth reacheth unto the skies.

Be thou exalted, O God, above the heavens:
And thy glory above all the earth.

ADORATION AND THANKSGIVING.

SIXTEENTH LESSON.

Ps. 113. PRAISE ye the Lord. Praise, O ye servants of the Lord,
Praise the name of the Lord.
Blessed be the name of the Lord from this time forth and for evermore.
From the rising of the sun unto the going down of the same the Lord's name is to be praised.
The Lord is high above all nations,
And his glory among the heavens.
Who is like unto the Lord our God, that hath his seat on high,
That humbleth himself to behold the things that are in heaven and in the earth?
He raiseth up the poor out of the dust,
And lifteth up the needy from the dunghill;
That he may set him with princes,
Even with the princes of his people.
He maketh the barren woman to keep house, *and to be* a joyful mother of children.
Praise ye the Lord.

Ps. 116. I LOVE the Lord, because he heareth my voice and my supplications.
Because he hath inclined his ear unto me, therefore will I call upon him as long as I live.
The chords of death compassed me, and the pains of Sheol gat hold upon me:
I found trouble and sorrow.
Then called I upon the name of the Lord;
O Lord, I beseech thee, deliver my soul.
Gracious is the Lord, and righteous;
Yea, our God is merciful.
The Lord preserveth the simple:
I was brought low, and he saved me.
Return unto thy rest, O my soul;
For the Lord hath dealt bountifully with thee.
For thou hast delivered my soul from death,
Mine eyes from tears, and my feet from falling.
I will walk before the Lord in the land of the living.
I believe, for I will speak:

I was greatly afflicted:
I said in my haste, all men are a lie.

What shall I render unto the Lord for all his benefits toward me?
I will take the cup of salvation, and call upon the name of the Lord.

I will pay my vows unto the Lord,
Yea, in the presence of all his people.

Precious in the sight of the Lord is the death of his saints.
O Lord, truly I am thy servant:

I am thy servant, the son of thine handmaid;
Thou hast loosed my bonds.

I will offer to thee the sacrifice of thanksgiving,
And I will call upon the name of the Lord.

I will pay vows unto the Lord,
Yea, in the presence of all his people:

In the courts of the Lord's house, in the midst of thee, O Jerusalem.
Praise ye the Lord.

SEVENTEENTH LESSON.

Ps. 148. PRAISE ye the Lord. Praise ye the Lord from the heavens:
Praise him in the heights.

Praise ye him, all his angels:
Praise ye him, all his host.

Praise ye him, sun and moon:
Praise him, all ye stars of light.

Praise him, ye heaven of heavens,
And ye waters that be above the heavens.

Let them praise the name of the Lord:
For he commanded, and they were created.

He hath also stablished them for ever and ever:
He hath made a decree which shall not pass away.

Praise the Lord from the earth,
Ye dragons, and all deeps:

Fire and hail, snow and vapor;
Stormy wind, fulfilling his word:

Mountains and all hills;
> *Fruitful trees and all cedars:*

Beasts and all cattle;
> *Creeping things and flying fowl:*

Kings of the earth and all peoples;
> *Princes and all judges of the earth:*

Both young men and maidens;
> *Old men and children:*

Let them praise the name of the Lord;
> *For his name alone is exalted:*

His glory is above the earth and heaven.
> *And he hath lifted up the horn of his people, the praise of all his saints;*

Even the children of Israel, a people near unto him.
> *Praise ye the Lord.*

Ps. 149. PRAISE ye the Lord. Sing unto the Lord a new song,
> *And his praise in the assembly of the saints.*

Let Israel rejoice in him that made him:
> *Let the children of Zion be joyful in their King.*

Let them praise his name in the dance:
> *Let them sing praises unto him with the timbrel and harp.*

For the Lord taketh pleasure in his people:
> *He will beautify the meek with salvation.*

Let the saints exult in glory:
> *Let them sing for joy upon their beds.*

Let the high praises of God *be* in their mouth,
> *And a two-edged sword in their hand;*

To execute vengeance upon the nations,
> *And punishments upon the peoples:*

To bind their kings with chains, and their nobles with fetters of iron;
> *To execute upon them the judgment written:*

This honor have all his saints.
> *Praise ye the Lord.*

ADORATION AND THANKSGIVING.

Ps. 150. PRAISE ye the Lord.   Praise God in his sanctuary:
Praise him in the firmament of his power.
Praise him for his mighty acts:
Praise him according to his excellent greatness.
Praise him with the sound of the trumpet:
Praise him with the psaltery and harp.
Praise him with the timbrel and dance:
Praise him with stringed instruments and the pipe.
Praise him upon the loud cymbals:
Praise him upon the high sounding cymbals.
Let every thing that hath breath praise the Lord.
Praise ye the Lord.

EIGHTEENTH LESSON.

Ps. 117. O PRAISE the Lord, all ye nations; laud him, all ye peoples.
For his mercy is great toward us.
And the truth of the Lord *endureth* for ever.
Praise ye the Lord.

Ps. 118. O GIVE thanks unto the Lord; for he is good: for his mercy *endureth* for ever.
Let Israel now say, That his mercy endureth for ever.
Let the house of Aaron now say, That his mercy *endureth* for ever.
Let them now that fear the Lord say, That his mercy endureth for ever.
Out of my distress I called upon the Lord:
The Lord answered me and set me in a large place.
The Lord is on my side; I will not fear:
What can man do unto me?
The Lord is on my side among them that help me:
Therefore shall I see my desire upon them that hate me.
It is better to trust in the Lord than to put confidence in man.
It is better to trust in the Lord than to put confidence in princes.
All nations compassed me about:
In the name of the Lord I will cut them off,
They compassed me about; yea, they compassed me about:
In the name of the Lord I will cut them off.

ADORATION AND THANKSGIVING.

They compassed me about like bees; they are quenched as the fire of thorns:
In the name of the Lord I will cut them off.

Thou didst thrust sore at me that I might fall:
But the Lord helped me.

The Lord is my strength and song;
And he is become my salvation.

The voice of rejoicing and salvation is in the tents of the righteous:
The right hand of the Lord doeth valiantly.

The right hand of the Lord is exalted:
The right hand of the Lord doeth valiantly.

I shall not die, but live,
And declare the works of the Lord.

The Lord has chastened me sore:
But he hath not given me over unto death.

Open to me the gates of righteousness:
I will enter into them, I will give thanks unto the Lord.

This is the gate of the Lord;
The righteous shall enter into it.

I will give thanks unto thee, for thou hast answered me,
And art become my salvation.

The stone which the builders rejected is become the head of the corner.
This is the Lord's doing; it is marvellous in our eyes.

This is the day which the Lord hath made;
We will rejoice and be glad in it.

Save now, we beseech thee, O Lord:
O Lord, we beseech thee, send now prosperity.

Blessed be he that cometh in the name of the Lord:
We have blessed you out of the house of the Lord.

The Lord is God, and he hath given us light:
Bind the sacrifice with cords, even unto the horns of the altar.

Thou art my God, and I will give thanks unto thee:
Thou art my God, I will exalt thee.

O give thanks unto the Lord; for he is good:
For his mercy endureth for ever.

NINETEENTH LESSON.

Ps. 24. The earth is the Lord's, and the fulness thereof;
The world, and they that dwell therein.

For he hath founded it upon the seas
And established it upon the floods.

Who shall ascend into the hill of the Lord?
And who shall stand in his holy place?

He that hath clean hands, and a pure heart; who hath not lifted up his soul unto vanity,
And hath not sworn deceitfully.

He shall receive a blessing from the Lord,
And righteousness from the God of his salvation.

This is the generation of them that seek after him,
That seek thy face, even Jacob.

Lift up your heads, O ye gates; and be ye lift up, ye everlasting doors:
And the King of glory shall come in.

Who is the King of glory?
The Lord strong and mighty, the Lord mighty in battle.

Lift up your heads, O ye gates; yea, lift them up, ye everlasting doors:
And the King of glory shall come in.

Who is this King of glory?
The Lord of hosts, he is the King of glory.

Ps. 47. O clap your hands, all ye peoples;
Shout unto God with the voice of triumph.

For the Lord Most High is terrible;
He is a great King over all the earth.

He shall subdue the peoples under us,
And the nations under our feet.

He shall choose our inheritance for us,
The glory of Jacob whom he loved.

God is gone up with a shout,
The Lord with the sound of a trumpet.

Sing praises to God, sing praises,
Sing praises unto our King, sing praises.

For God is the King of all the earth:
Sing ye praises with understanding.
God reigneth over the nations:
God sitteth upon his holy throne.
The princes of the peoples are gathered together *to be* the people of the God of Abraham;
For the shields of the earth belong unto God; he is greatly exalted.

Ps. 135.   PRAISE ye the Lord.   Praise ye the name of the Lord;
Praise him, O ye servants of the Lord:
Ye that stand in the house of the Lord,
In the courts of the house of our God.
Praise ye the Lord; for the Lord is good:
Sing praises unto his name: for it is pleasant.
For the Lord hath chosen Jacob unto himself,
And Israel for his own possession.
For I know that the Lord is great,
And that our Lord is above all gods.
The idols of the nations are silver and gold,
The work of men's hands.
They have mouths, but they speak not;
Eyes have they, but they see not:
They have ears, but they hear not;
Neither is there any breath in their mouths.
They that make them shall be like unto them;
Yea, every one that trusteth in them.
O house of Israel, bless ye the Lord:
O house of Aaron, bless ye the Lord:
O house of Levi, bless ye the Lord:
Ye that fear the Lord, bless ye the Lord.
Blessed be the Lord out of Zion, who dwelleth at Jerusalem.
Praise ye the Lord.

THE MAJESTY AND HOLINESS OF GOD.

TWENTIETH LESSON.

Ps. 89. I WILL sing of the mercies of the Lord for ever:
    With my mouth will I make known thy faithfulness to all generations.
For I have said, Mercy shall be built up for ever;
    Thy faithfulness shalt thou establish in the very heavens.
I have made a covenant with my chosen,
    I have sworn unto David my servant;
Thy seed will I establish for ever,
    And build up thy throne to all generations.
And the heavens shall praise thy wonders, O Lord;
    Thy faithfulness also in the assembly of the holy ones.
For who in the skies can be compared unto the Lord?
    Who among the sons of the mighty is like unto the Lord,
A God very terrible in the council of the holy ones,
    And to be feared above all them that are round about him?
O Lord God of hosts, who is a mighty one, like unto thee, O Jehovah?
    And thy faithfulness is round about thee.
Thou rulest the pride of the sea:
    When the waves thereof arise, thou stillest them.
Thou hast broken Rahab in pieces, as one that is slain;
    Thou hast scattered thine enemies with the arm of thy strength.
The heavens are thine, the earth also is thine:
    The world and the fulness thereof, thou hast founded them.
The north and the south, thou hast created them:
    Tabor and Hermon rejoice in thy name.
Thou hast a mighty arm:
    Strong is thy hand, and high is thy right hand.
Righteousness and justice are the foundation of thy throne:
    Mercy and truth go before thy face.
Blessed is the people that know the joyful sound:
    They walk, O Lord, in the light of thy countenance.
In thy name do they rejoice all the day:
    And in thy righteousness are they exalted.
For thou art the glory of their strength:
    And in thy favor our horn shall be exalted.

THE MAJESTY AND HOLINESS OF GOD.

For our shield belongeth unto the Lord;
And our king to the Holy One of Israel.

Ps. 93. THE Lord reigneth; he is clothed with majesty;
Jehovah is clothed with strength; he hath girded himself therewith.

The world also is established, that it cannot be moved.
Thy throne is established of old: thou art from everlasting.

The floods have lifted up, O Lord, the floods have lifted up their voice;
The floods lift up their waves.

Above the voices of many waters, the mighty breakers of the sea,
The Lord on high is mighty.

Thy testimonies are very sure:
Holiness becometh thine house, O Lord, for evermore.

TWENTY-FIRST LESSON.

Ps. 8. O LORD, our Lord, how excellent is thy name in all the earth!
Who hast set thy glory upon the heavens.

Out of the mouth of babes and sucklings hast thou established strength,
Because of thine adversaries, that thou mightest still the enemy and the avenger.

When I consider thy heavens, the work of thy fingers,
The moon and the stars, which thou hast ordained;

What is man, that thou art mindful of him?
And the son of man, that thou visitest him?

For thou hast made him but little lower than God,
And crownest him with glory and honor.

Thou madest him to have dominion over the works of thy hands;
Thou hast put all things under his feet:

All sheep and oxen, yea, and the beasts of the field;
The fowl of the air, and the fish of the sea,

Whatsoever passeth through the paths of the seas.
O Lord, our Lord, how excellent is thy name in all the earth!

Ps. 96. O SING unto the Lord a new song:
Sing unto the Lord, all the earth.

THE MAJESTY AND HOLINESS OF GOD.

Sing unto the Lord, bless his name;
Shew forth his salvation from day to day.
Declare his glory among the nations,
His marvellous works among all the peoples.
For great is the Lord, and highly to be praised:
He is to be feared above all gods.
For all the gods of the peoples are idols:
But the Lord made the heavens.
Honor and majesty are before him:
Strength and beauty are in his sanctuary.
Give unto the Lord, ye kindreds of the peoples,
Give unto the Lord glory and strength.
Give unto the Lord the glory due unto his name:
Bring an offering, and come into his courts.
O worship the Lord in the beauty of holiness:
Tremble before him, all the earth.
Say among the nations, The Lord reigneth: the world also is stablished that it cannot be moved:
He shall judge the peoples with equity.
Let the heavens be glad, and let the earth rejoice;
Let the sea roar, and the fulness thereof;
Let the field exult, and all that is therein;
Then shall all the trees of the wood sing for joy;
Before the Lord, for he cometh;
For he cometh to judge the earth:
He shall judge the world with righteousness,
And the peoples with his truth.

TWENTY-SECOND LESSON.

Ps. 97. THE Lord reigneth; let the earth rejoice;
Let the multitude of isles be glad.

Clouds and darkness are round about him:
Righteousness and justice are the foundation of his throne.

A fire goeth before him, and burneth up his adversaries round about.
His lightnings lightened the world.

The earth saw, and trembled. The mountains melted like wax at the presence of the Lord,
At the presence of the Lord of the whole earth.

The heavens declare his righteousness,
And all the peoples have seen his glory.

Ashamed be all they that serve graven images, that boast themselves of idols:
Worship him, all ye gods.

Zion heard and was glad, and the daughters of Judah rejoiced;
Because of thy judgments, O Lord.

For thou, Lord, art most high above all the earth:
Thou art exalted far above all gods.

O ye that love the Lord, hate evil:
He preserveth the souls of his saints;

He delivereth them out of the hand of the wicked.
Light is sown for the righteous, and gladness for the upright in heart.

Be glad in the Lord, ye righteous;
And give thanks to his holy name.

Ps. 99. THE Lord reigneth; let the people tremble:
He sitteth upon the cherubim; let the earth be moved.

The Lord is great in Zion;
And he is high above all the peoples.

Let them praise thy great and terrible name:
Holy is he.

The king's strength also loveth justice; thou dost establish equity,
Thou executest justice and righteousness in Jacob.

Exalt ye the Lord our God, and worship at his footstool:
Holy is he.

THE MAJESTY AND HOLINESS OF GOD.

Moses and Aaron among his priests, and Samuel among them that call upon his name;
They called upon the Lord, and he answered them.

He spake unto them in the pillar of cloud:
They kept his testimonies, and the statute that he gave them.

Thou answeredst them, O Lord our God: thou wast a God that forgavest them,
Though thou tookest vengeance of their doings.

Exalt ye the Lord our God, and worship at his holy hill;
For the Lord our God is holy.

TWENTY-THIRD LESSON.

Ps. 33. REJOICE in the Lord, O ye righteous:
Praise is comely for the upright.

Give thanks unto the Lord with harp:
Sing praises unto him with the psaltery of ten strings.

Sing unto him a new song;
Play skillfully with a loud noise.

For the word of the Lord is right;
And all his work is done in faithfulness.

He loveth righteousness and justice:
The earth is full of the loving-kindness of the Lord.

By the word of the Lord were the heavens made;
And all of the host of them by the breath of his mouth.

He gathereth the waters of the sea together as an heap:
He layeth up the deeps in storehouses.

Let all the earth fear the Lord:
Let all the inhabitants of the world stand in awe of him.

For he spake, and it was done;
He commanded, and it stood fast.

The Lord bringeth the counsel of the nations to naught:
He maketh the thoughts of the peoples to be of none effect.

The counsel of the Lord standeth fast for ever,
The thoughts of his heart to all generations.

Blessed is the nation whose God is the Lord;
The people whom he hath chosen for his own inheritance.

The Lord looketh from heaven;
He beholdeth all the sons of men;

From the place of his habitation he looketh forth upon all the inhabitants of the earth;
He that fashioneth the hearts of them all, that considereth all their works.

There is no king saved by the multitude of an host:
A mighty man is not delivered by great strength.

An horse is a vain thing for safety:
Neither shall he deliver any by his great power.

Behold, the eye of the Lord is upon them that fear him,
Upon them that hope in his mercy;

To deliver their soul from death,
And to keep them alive in famine.

Our soul hath waited for the Lord:
He is our help and our shield.

For our heart shall rejoice in him,
Because we have trusted in his holy name.

Let thy mercy, O Lord, be upon us,
According as we have hoped in thee.

Ps. III. PRAISE ye the Lord. I will give thanks unto the Lord with my whole heart,
In the council of the upright, and in the congregation.

The works of the Lord are great,
Sought out of all them that have pleasure therein.

His work is honor and majesty: and his righteousness endureth for ever.
He hath made his wonderful works to be remembered:

The Lord is gracious and full of compassion. He hath given meat unto them that fear him:
He will ever be mindful of his covenant.

He hath shewed his people the power of his works,
In giving them the heritage of the nations.

The works of his hands are truth and judgment;
All his precepts are sure.

They are established for ever and ever,
They are done in truth and uprightness.

He hath sent redemption unto his people; he hath commanded his covenant for ever:
Holy and reverend is his name.

The fear of the Lord is the beginning of wisdom; a good understanding have all they that do his commandments:
His praise endureth for ever.

TWENTY-FOURTH LESSON.

Ps. 104. BLESS the Lord, O my soul.
O Lord my God, thou art very great;
Thou art clothed with honor and majesty.
Who coverest thyself with light as with a garment;
Who stretchest out the heavens like a curtain:
Who layeth the beams of his chambers in the waters;
Who maketh the clouds his chariot;
Who walketh upon the wings of the wind:
Who maketh winds his messengers;
Flames of fire his ministers:
Who laid the foundations of the earth,
That it should not be moved for ever.
Thou coveredst it with the deep as with a vesture;
The waters stood above the mountains.
At thy rebuke they fled;
At the voice of thy thunder they hasted away;
The mountains rose, the valleys sank,
Unto the place which thou hadst founded for them.
Thou hast set a bound that they may not pass over;
That they turn not again to cover the earth.
He sendeth forth springs into the valleys;
They run among the mountains:
They give drink to every beast of the field;
The wild asses quench their thirst.

GOD'S GLORY IN NATURE.

By them the fowl of the heaven have their habitation,
  They sing among the branches.
He watereth the mountains from his chambers:
  The earth is satisfied with the fruit of thy works.
He causeth the grass to grow for the cattle,
  And herb for the service of man;
That he may bring forth food out of the earth:
  And wine that maketh glad the heart of man,
And oil to make his face to shine,
  And bread that strengtheneth man's heart.
The trees of the Lord are filled with moisture:
  The cedars of Lebanon, which he hath planted;
Where the birds make their nests:
  As for the stork, the fir trees are her house.
The high mountains are for the wild goats;
  The rocks are a refuge for the conies.
He appointed the moon for seasons:
  The sun knoweth his going down.
Thou makest darkness, and it is night;
  Wherein all the beasts of the forest do creep forth.
The young lions roar after their prey,
  And seek their meat from God.
The sun ariseth, they get them away, and lay them down in their dens.
  Man goeth forth unto his work and to his labor until the evening.
O Lord, how manifold are thy works! in wisdom hast thou made them all:
  The earth is full of thy riches.
There is the sea, great and wide,
  Wherein are things creeping innumerable, both small and great beasts.
There go the ships;
  There is leviathan, whom thou hast formed to take his pastime therein.
These wait all upon thee,
  That thou mayest give them their meat in due season.
That thou givest unto them they gather;
  Thou openest thine hand, they are satisfied with good.

Thou hidest thy face, they are troubled;
Thou takest away their breath, they die, and return to their dust.

Thou sendest forth thy spirit, they are created;
And thou renewest the face of the ground.

Let the glory of the Lord endure for ever;
Let the Lord rejoice in his works:

Who looketh on the earth, and it trembleth;
He toucheth the mountains, and they smoke.

I will sing unto the Lord as long as I live:
I will sing praise to my God while I have any being.

Let my meditation be sweet unto him:
I will rejoice in the Lord.

Let sinners be consumed out of the earth,
And let the wicked be no more.

Bless the Lord, O my soul.
Praise ye the Lord.

TWENTY-FIFTH LESSON.

Ps. 139. O Lord, thou hast searched me, and known *me.*
Thou knowest my downsitting and mine uprising,

Thou understandest my thought afar off.
Thou searchest out my path and my lying down,

And art acquainted with all my ways.
For there is not a word in my tongue, but, lo, O Lord, thou knowest it altogether.

Thou hast beset me behind and before,
And laid thine hand upon me.

Such knowledge is too wonderful for me;
It is high, I cannot attain unto it.

Whither shall I go from thy spirit?
Or whither shall I flee from thy presence?

If I ascend up into heaven, thou art there:
If I make my bed in Sheol, behold, thou art there.

If I take the wings of the morning,
And dwell in the uttermost parts of the sea;

Even there shall thy hand lead me,
  And thy right hand shall hold me.
If I say, Surely the darkness shall overwhelm me,
  And the light about me shall be night:
Even the darkness hideth not from thee, but the night shineth as the day:
  The darkness and the light are both alike to thee.
For thou didst form my reins:
  Thou didst cover me in my mother's womb.
I will give thanks unto thee; for I am fearfully and wonderfully made:
  Wonderful are thy works; and that my soul knoweth right well.
My frame was not hidden from thee, when I was made in secret,
  And curiously wrought in the lowest parts of the earth.
Thine eyes did see mine unperfect substance,
  And in thy book were all my members written,
Which day by day were fashioned,
  When as yet there was none of them.
How precious also are thy thoughts unto me, O God!
  How great is the sum of them!
If I should count them, they are more in number than the sand:
  When I awake, I am still with thee.
Surely thou wilt slay the wicked, O God:
  Depart from me therefore, ye bloodthirsty men.
For they speak against thee wickedly,
  And thine enemies take thy name in vain.
Do not I hate them, O Lord, that hate thee?
  And am not I grieved with those that rise up against thee?
I hate them with perfect hatred:
  They are become mine enemies.
Search me, O God, and know my heart:
  Try me, and know my thoughts:
And see if there be any way of wickedness in me,
  And lead me in the way everlasting.

TWENTY-SIXTH LESSON.

Ps. 18. I LOVE thee, O Lord, my strength.
The Lord is my rock, and my fortress, and my deliverer;
My God, my strong rock, in him will I trust;
My shield, and the horn of my salvation, my high tower.
I will call upon the Lord, who is worthy to be praised:
So shall I be saved from mine enemies.
The cords of death compassed me,
And the floods of ungodliness made me afraid.
The cords of Sheol were round about me:
The snares of death came upon me.
In my distress I called upon the Lord,
And cried unto my God:
He heard my voice out of his temple,
And my cry before him came into his ears.
Then the earth shook and trembled,
The foundations also of the mountains quaked and were shaken, because he was wroth.
There went up a smoke out of his nostrils, and fire out of his mouth devoured:
Coals were kindled by it.
He bowed the heavens also, and came down;
And thick darkness was under his feet.
And he rode upon a cherub, and did fly:
Yea, he flew swiftly upon the wings of the wind.
He made darkness his hiding place, his pavilion round about him;
Darkness of waters, thick clouds of the skies.
At the brightness before him his thick clouds passed,
Hailstones and coals of fire.
The Lord also thundered in the heavens, and the Most High uttered his voice;
Hailstones and coals of fire.
And he sent out his arrows, and scattered them;
Yea, lightnings manifold, and discomfited them.
Then the channels of waters appeared,
And the foundations of the world were laid bare,

At thy rebuke, O Lord,
At the blast of the breath of thy nostrils.

He sent from on high, he took me:
He drew me out of many waters.

He delivered me from my strong enemy,
And from them that hated me, for they were too mighty for me.

As for God, his way is perfect: the word of the Lord is tried;
He is a shield unto all them that trust in him.

For who is God, save the Lord?
And who is a rock, beside our God?

The God that girdeth me with strength,
And maketh my way perfect.

He maketh my feet like hinds' *feet:*
And setteth me upon my high places.

He teacheth my hands to war;
So that mine arms do bend a bow of brass.

Thou hast also given me the shield of thy salvation: and thy right hand hath holden me up,
And thy gentleness hath made me great.

TWENTY-SEVENTH LESSON.

JOB 36: 26. BEHOLD, God is great, and we know him not;
The number of his years is unsearchable.

For he draweth up the drops of water,
Which distil in rain from his vapor:

Which the skies pour down
And drop upon man abundantly.

Yea, can any understand the spreadings of the clouds,
The thunderings of his pavilion?

Behold, he spreadeth his light around him;
And he covereth the bottom of the sea.

For by these he judgeth the peoples;
He giveth meat in abundance.

He covereth his hands with the lightning;
And giveth it a charge that it strike the mark.
The noise thereof telleth concerning him,
The cattle also concerning the storm that cometh up.

JOB 37. Yea, at this also my heart trembleth,
And is moved out of its place.
Hear, oh, hear the noise of his voice,
And the sound that goeth out of his mouth.
He sendeth it forth under the whole heaven,
And his lightning unto the ends of the earth.
After it a voice roareth;
He thundereth with the voice of his majesty: and he stayeth them not when his voice is heard.
God thundereth marvellously with his voice;
Great things doeth he, which we cannot comprehend.
For he saith to the snow, Fall thou on the earth;
Likewise to the shower of rain, and to the showers of his mighty rain.
He sealeth up the hand of every man;
That all men whom he hath made may know it.
Then the beasts go into coverts,
And remain in their dens.
Out of the chamber *of the south* cometh the storm:
And cold out of the north.
By the breath of God ice is given:
And the breadth of the waters is straitened.
Yea, he ladeth the thick cloud with moisture;
He spreadeth abroad the cloud of his lightning:
And it is turned round about by his guidance,
That they may do whatsoever he commandeth them upon the face of the habitable world:
Whether it be for correction, or for his land,
Or for mercy, that he cause it to come.
Hearken unto this, O Job:
Stand still, and consider the wondrous works of God.
Dost thou know how God layeth *his charge* upon them,
And causeth the lightning of his cloud to shine?

Dost thou know the balancings of the clouds,
   The wondrous works of him which is perfect in knowledge?
How thy garments are warm,
   When the earth is still by reason of the south wind?
Canst thou with him spread out the sky,
   Which is strong as a molten mirror?
Teach us what we shall say unto him;
   For we cannot order our speech by reason of darkness.
Shall it be told him that I would speak?
   Or should a man wish that he were swallowed up?
And now men see not the light which is bright in the skies:
   But the wind passeth, and cleareth them.
Out of the north cometh golden splendor:
   God hath upon him terrible majesty.
Touching the Almighty, we cannot find him out; he is excellent in power:
   And in judgment and plenteous justice he will not afflict.
Men do therefore fear him:
   He regardeth not any that are wise of heart.

TWENTY-EIGHTH LESSON.

JOB 38. THEN the Lord answered Job out of the whirlwind, and said,
   Who is this that darkeneth counsel by words without knowledge?
Gird up now thy loins like a man;
   For I will demand of thee, and declare thou unto me.
Where wast thou when I laid the foundations of the earth?
   Declare, if thou hast understanding.
Who determined the measures thereof, if thou knowest?
   Or who stretched the line upon it?
Whereupon were the foundations thereof fastened?
   Or who laid the corner stone thereof;
When the morning stars sang together,
   And all the sons of God shouted for joy?
Or *who* shut up the sea with doors,
   When it brake forth, as if it had issued out of the womb;

When I made the cloud the garment thereof,
  And thick darkness a swaddlingband for it,
And marked out for it my bound,
  And set bars and doors,
And said, Hitherto shalt thou come, but no further:
  And here shall thy proud waves be stayed?
Hast thou commanded the morning since thy days *began,*
  And caused the dayspring to know its place;
That it might take hold of the ends of the earth,
  And the wicked be shaken out of it?
It is changed as clay under the seal;
  And all things stand forth as a garment:
And from the wicked their light is withholden,
  And the high arm is broken.
Hast thou entered into the springs of the sea?
  Or hast thou walked in the recesses of the deep?
Have the gates of death been revealed unto thee?
  Or hast thou seen the gates of the shadow of death?
Hast thou comprehended the earth in its breadth?
  Declare, if thou knowest it all.
Where is the way to the dwelling of light,
  And as for darkness, where is the place thereof;
That thou shouldst take it to the bound thereof,
  And that thou shouldest discern the paths to the house thereof?
Doubtless, thou knowest, for thou wast then born,
  And the number of thy days is great!
Hast thou entered the treasuries of the snow,
  Or hast thou seen the treasuries of the hail,
Which I have reserved against the time of trouble,
  Against the day of battle and war?
By what way is the light parted,
  Or the east wind scattered upon the earth?
Who hath cleft a channel for the waterflood,
  Or a way for the lightning of the thunder;
To cause it to rain on a land where no man is;
  On the wilderness, wherein there is no man;

To satisfy the waste and desolate ground;
  And to cause the tender grass to spring forth?

Hath the rain a father?
  Or who hath begotten the drops of dew?

Who can number the clouds by wisdom?
  Or who can pour out the bottles of heaven,

When the dust runneth into a mass,
  And the clods cleave fast together?

Wilt thou hunt the prey for the lioness?
  Or satisfy the appetite of the young lions,

When they couch in their dens,
  And abide in the covert to lie in wait?

Who provideth for the raven his prey, when his young ones cry unto God,
  And wander for lack of meat?

TWENTY-NINTH LESSON.

Ps. 19. THE heavens declare the glory of God;
  And the firmament sheweth his handywork.

Day unto day uttereth speech,
  And night unto night sheweth knowledge.

There is no speech nor language;
  Their voice cannot be heard.

Their line is gone out through all the earth,
  And their words to the end of the world.

In them hath he set a tabernacle for the sun, which is as a bridegroom coming out of his chamber,
  And rejoiceth as a strong man to run his course.

His going forth is from the end of the heaven, and his circuit unto the ends of it:
  And there is nothing hid from the heat thereof.

The law of the Lord is perfect, restoring the soul:
  The testimony of the Lord is sure, making wise the simple.

The precepts of the Lord are right, rejoicing the heart:
  The commandment of the Lord is pure, enlightening the eyes.

The fear of the Lord is clean, enduring for ever:
  The judgments of the Lord are true, and righteous altogether.
More to be desired are they than gold, yea, than much fine gold:
  Sweeter also than honey and the honeycomb.
Moreover by them is thy servant warned:
  In keeping of them there is great reward.
Who can discern *his* errors?
  Clear thou me from hidden faults.
Keep back thy servant also from presumptuous *sins;*
  Let them not have dominion over me: then shall I be perfect, and I shall be clear from great transgression.
Let the words of my mouth and the meditation of my heart be acceptable in thy sight,
  O Lord, my rock, and my redeemer.

Ps. 29. GIVE unto the Lord, O ye sons of the mighty,
  Give unto the Lord glory and strength.
Give unto the Lord the glory due unto his name;
  Worship the Lord in the beauty of holiness.
The voice of the Lord is upon the waters:
  The God of glory thundereth, even the Lord upon many waters.
The voice of the Lord is powerful;
  The voice of the Lord is full of majesty.
The voice of the Lord breaketh the cedars;
  Yea, the Lord breaketh in pieces the cedars of Lebanon.
He maketh them also to skip like a calf;
  Lebanon and Sirion like a young wild-ox.
The voice of the Lord cleaveth the flames of fire.
  The voice of the Lord shaketh the wilderness: the Lord shaketh the wildernes of Kadesh.
The voice of the Lord maketh the hinds to calve, and strippeth the forests bare:
  And in his temple every thing saith, Glory.
The Lord sat *as king* at the Flood;
  Yea, the Lord sitteth as king for ever.
The Lord will give strength unto his people;
  The Lord will bless his people with peace.

THIRTIETH LESSON.

Ps. 107. O GIVE thanks unto the Lord; for he is good;
For his mercy endureth for ever.
Let the redeemed of the Lord say so,
Whom he hath redeemed from the hand of the adversary;
And gathered them out of the lands,
From the east and from the west, from the north and from the south.
They wandered in the wilderness in a desert way; they found no city of habitation.
Hungry and thirsty, their soul fainted in them.
Then they cried unto the Lord in their trouble,
And he delivered them out of their distresses.
He led them also by a straight way,
That they might go to a city of habitation.
Oh that men would praise the Lord for his goodness,
And for his wonderful works to the children of men!
For he satisfieth the longing soul,
And the hungry soul he filleth with good.
Such as sat in darkness and in the shadow of death,
Being bound in affliction and iron;
Because they rebelled against the words of God,
And contemned the counsel of the Most High:
Therefore he brought down their heart with labor;
They fell down, and there was none to help.
Then they cried unto the Lord in their trouble,
And he saved them out of their distresses.
He brought them out of darkness and the shadow of death,
And brake their bands in sunder.
Oh that men would praise the Lord for his goodness,
And for his wonderful works to the children of men!
For he hath broken the gates of brass,
And cut the bars of iron in sunder.
Fools because of their transgression,
And because of their iniquities, are afflicted.

Their soul abhorreth all manner of meat;
   And they draw near unto the gates of death.
Then they cry unto the Lord in their trouble,
   And he saveth them out of their distresses.
He sendeth his word, and healeth them,
   And delivereth them from their destructions.
Oh that men would praise the Lord for his goodness,
   And for his wonderful works to the children of men!
And let them offer the sacrifices of thanksgiving,
   And declare his works with singing.
They that go down to the sea in ships,
   That do business in great waters;
These see the works of the Lord,
   And his wonders in the deep.
For he commandeth, and raiseth the stormy wind,
   Which lifteth up the waves thereof.
They mount up to the heaven, they go down again to the depths:
   Their soul melteth away because of trouble.
They reel to and fro, and stagger like a drunken man,
   And are at their wits' end.
Then they cry unto the Lord in their trouble,
   And he bringeth them out of their distresses.
He maketh the storm a calm,
   So that the waves thereof are still.
Then are they glad because they be quiet;
   So he bringeth them unto their desired haven.
Oh that men would praise the Lord for his goodness,
   And for his wonderful works to the children of men!

THIRTY-FIRST LESSON.

Ps. 23. The Lord is my shepherd; I shall not want.
He maketh me to lie down in green pastures:
He leadeth me beside the still waters.
He restoreth my soul:
He guideth me in the paths of righteousness for his name's sake.
Yea, though I walk through the valley of the shadow of death,
I will fear no evil; for thou art with me:
Thy rod and thy staff, they comfort me.
Thou preparest a table before me in the presence of mine enemies:
Thou hast anointed my head with oil; my cup runneth over.
Surely goodness and mercy shall follow me all the days of my life:
And I will dwell in the house of the Lord for ever.

Ps. 91. He that dwelleth in the secret place of the Most High
Shall abide under the shadow of the Almighty.
I will say of the Lord, He is my refuge and my fortress;
My God, in whom I trust.
For he shall deliver thee from the snare of the fowler,
And from the noisome pestilence.
He shall cover thee with his pinions, and under his wings shalt thou take refuge:
His truth is a shield and a buckler.
Thou shalt not be afraid for the terror by night,
Nor for the arrow that flieth by day;
For the pestilence that walketh in darkness,
Nor for the destruction that wasteth at noonday.
A thousand shall fall at thy side,
And ten thousand at thy right hand;
But it shall not come nigh thee.
Only with thine eyes shalt thou behold, and see the reward of the wicked.
For thou, O Lord, art my refuge!
Thou hast made the Most High thy habitation;
There shall no evil befall thee,
Neither shall any plague come nigh thy tent.

GOD'S GLORY IN PROVIDENCE AND GRACE.

For he shall give his angels charge over thee,
  To keep thee in all thy ways.
They shall bear thee up in their hands,
  Lest thou dash thy foot against a stone.
Thou shalt tread upon the lion and adder:
  The young lion and the serpent shalt thou trample under feet.
Because he hath set his love upon me, therefore will I deliver him:
  I will set him on high, because he hath known my name.
He shall call upon me, and I will answer him; I will be with him in trouble:
  I will deliver him, and honor him.
With long life will I satisfy him,
  And shew him my salvation.

THIRTY-SECOND LESSON.

Ps. 65. PRAISE waiteth for thee, O God, in Zion:
  And unto thee shall the vow be performed.
O thou that hearest prayer,
  Unto thee shall all flesh come.
Iniquities prevail against me:
  As for our transgressions, thou shalt forgive them.
Blessed is the man whom thou choosest, and causest to approach *unto thee*,
      that he may dwell in thy courts:
  We shall be satisfied with the goodness of thy house, thy holy temple.
By terrible things thou wilt answer us in righteousness,
  O God of our salvation;
Thou that art the confidence of all the ends of the earth,
  And of them that are afar off upon the sea:
Which by his strength setteth fast the mountains;
  Being girded about with might:
Which stilleth the roaring of the seas, the roaring of their waves,
  And the tumult of the peoples.
They also that dwell in the uttermost parts are afraid at thy tokens:
  Thou makest the outgoings of the morning and evening to rejoice.

GOD'S GLORY IN PROVIDENCE AND GRACE.

Thou visitest the earth, and waterest it, thou greatly enrichest it;
The river of God is full of water:

Thou providest them corn, when thou hast so prepared the earth.
Thou waterest her furrows abundantly;

Thou settlest the ridges thereof:
Thou makest it soft with showers; thou blessest the springing thereof.

Thou crownest the year with thy goodness;
And thy paths drop fatness.

They drop upon the pastures of the wilderness:
And the hills are girded with joy.

The pastures are clothed with flocks; the valleys also are covered over with corn;
They shout for joy, they also sing.

Ps. 125. THEY that trust in the Lord
Are as mount Zion, which cannot be moved, but abideth for ever.

As the mountains are round about Jerusalem, so the Lord is round about his people,
From this time forth and for evermore.

For the sceptre of wickedness shall not rest upon the lot of the righteous;
That the righteous put not forth their hands unto iniquity.

Do good, O Lord, unto those that be good, and to them that are upright in their hearts.
But as for such as turn aside unto their crooked ways,

The Lord shall lead them forth with the workers of iniquity.
Peace be upon Israel.

THIRTY-THIRD LESSON.

Ps. 121. I WILL lift up mine eyes unto the mountains:
From whence shall my help come?

My help *cometh* from the Lord,
Which made heaven and earth.

He will not suffer thy foot to be moved:
He that keepeth thee will not slumber.

Behold, he that keepeth Israel
   Shall neither slumber nor sleep.
The Lord is thy keeper:
   The Lord is thy shade upon thy right hand.
The sun shall not smite thee by day,
   Nor the moon by night.
The Lord shall keep thee from all evil;
   He shall keep thy soul.
The Lord shall keep thy going out and thy coming in,
   From this time forth and for evermore.

Ps. 127. EXCEPT the Lord build the house,
   They labor in vain that build it:
Except the Lord keep the city,
   The watchman waketh but in vain.
It is vain for you that ye rise early, and so late take rest, and eat the bread of toil:
   For so he giveth unto his beloved sleep.
Lo, children are an heritage of the Lord:
   And the fruit of the womb is his reward.
As arrows in the hand of a mighty man,
   So are the children of youth.
Happy is the man that hath his quiver full of them:
   They shall not be ashamed, when they speak with their enemies in the gate.

Ps. 146. PRAISE ye the Lord.
   Praise the Lord, O my soul.
While I live will I praise the Lord:
   I will sing praises unto my God while I have any being.
Put not your trust in princes,
   Nor in the son of man, in whom there is no help.
His breath goeth forth, he returneth to his earth;
   In that very day his thoughts perish.
Happy is he that hath the God of Jacob for his help,
   Whose hope is in the Lord his God:
Which made heaven and earth,
   The sea, and all that in them is:

Which keepeth truth for ever:
: *Which executeth judgment for the oppressed;*
Which giveth food to the hungry ·
: *The Lord looseth the prisoners;*
The Lord openeth *the eyes of* the blind;
: *The Lord raiseth up them that are bowed down;*
The Lord loveth the righteous;
: *The Lord preserveth the strangers;*
He upholdeth the fatherless and widow;
: *But the way of the wicked he turneth upside down.*
The Lord shall reign for ever, thy God, O Zion, unto all generations.
: *Praise ye the Lord.*

THIRTY-FOURTH LESSON.

Ps. 34. I will bless the Lord at all times:
: *His praise shall continually be in my mouth.*
My soul shall make her boast in the Lord:
: *The meek shall hear thereof, and be glad.*
O magnify the Lord with me,
: *And let us exalt his name together.*
I sought the Lord, and he answered me,
: *And delivered me from all my fears.*
They looked unto him, and were lightened:
: *And their faces shall never be confounded.*
This poor man cried, and the Lord heard him,
: *And saved him out of all his troubles.*
The angel of the Lord encampeth round about them that fear him,
: *And delivereth them.*
O taste and see that the Lord is good:
: *Blessed is the man that trusteth in him.*
O fear the Lord, ye his saints:
: *For there is no want to them that fear him.*
The young lions do lack, and suffer hunger:
: *But they that seek the Lord shall not want any good thing.*

GOD'S GLORY IN PROVIDENCE AND GRACE.

Come, ye children, hearken unto me:
I will teach you the fear of the Lord.

What man is he that desireth life,
And loveth many days, that he may see good?

Keep thy tongue from evil,
And thy lips from speaking guile.

Depart from evil, and do good;
Seek peace, and pursue it.

The eyes of the Lord are toward the righteous,
And his ears are open unto their cry.

The face of the Lord is against them that do evil,
To cut off the remembrance of them from the earth.

The righteous cried, and the Lord heard,
And delivered them out of all their troubles.

The Lord is nigh unto them that are of a broken heart,
And saveth such as be of a contrite spirit.

Many are the afflictions of the righteous:
But the Lord delivereth him out of them all.

He keepeth all his bones:
Not one of them is broken.

Evil shall slay the wicked:
And they that hate the righteous shall be condemned.

The Lord redeemeth the soul of his servants:
And none of them that trust in him shall be condemned.

THIRTY-FIFTH LESSON.

Ps. 105. O GIVE thanks unto the Lord, call upon his name;
Make known his doings among the peoples.

Sing unto him, sing praises unto him;
Talk ye of all his marvellous works.

Glory ye in his holy name:
Let the heart of them rejoice that seek the Lord.

Seek ye the Lord and his strength;
Seek his face evermore.

Remember his marvellous works that he hath done;
  His wonders, and the judgments of his mouth;
O ye seed of Abraham his servant,
  Ye children of Jacob, his chosen ones.
He is the Lord our God:
  His judgments are in all the earth.
He hath remembered his covenant for ever,
  The word which he commanded to a thousand generations;
The covenant which he made with Abraham,
  And his oath unto Isaac;
And confirmed the same unto Jacob for a statute,
  To Israel for an everlasting covenant:
Saying, Unto thee will I give the land of Canaan,
  The lot of your inheritance:
When they were but a few men in number;
  Yea, very few, and sojourners in it:
And they went about from nation to nation,
  From one kingdom to another people.
He suffered no man to do them wrong;
  Yea, he reproved kings for their sakes;
Saying, Touch not mine anointed ones,
  And do my prophets no harm.
And he called for a famine upon the land;
  He brake the whole staff of bread.
He sent a man before them;
  Joseph was sold for a servant:
His feet they hurt with fetters;
  He was laid in chains of iron:
Until the time that his word came to pass;
  The word of the Lord tried him.
The king sent and loosed him;
  Even the ruler of peoples, and let him go free.
He made him lord of his house,
  And ruler of all his substance:
To bind his princes at his pleasure,
  And teach his senators wisdom.

Israel also came into Egypt;
  And Jacob sojourned in the land of Ham.
And he increased his people greatly,
  And made them stronger than their adversaries.
He turned their heart to hate his people,
  To deal subtilly with his servants.
He sent Moses his servant,
  And Aaron whom he had chosen.
They set among them his signs,
  And wonders in the land of Ham.
Egypt was glad when they departed;
  For the fear of them had fallen upon them.
He spread a cloud for a covering;
  And fire to give light in the night.
They asked, and he brought quails,
  And satisfied them with the bread of heaven.
He opened the rock, and waters gushed out;
  They ran in dry places like a river.
For he remembered his holy word,
  And Abraham his servant.
And he brought forth his people with joy,
  And his chosen with singing.
And he gave them the lands of the nations:
  And they took the labor of the peoples in possession:
That they might keep his statutes, and observe his laws.
  Praise ye the Lord.

THIRTY-SIXTH LESSON.

Ps. 144. BLESSED be the Lord my rock,
  Which teacheth my hands to war, and my fingers to fight:
My loving-kindness, and my fortress,
  My high tower, and my deliverer;
My shield, and he in whom I trust;
  Who subdueth my people under me.

Lord, what is man, that thou takest knowledge of him?
Or the son of man, that thou makest account of him?

Man is like to vanity:
His days are as a shadow that passeth away.

Bow thy heavens, O Lord, and come down:
Touch the mountains, and they shall smoke.

Cast forth lightning, and scatter them:
Send out thine arrows, and discomfit them.

Stretch forth thine hand from above;
Rescue me, and deliver me out of great waters,

Out of the hand of aliens;
Whose mouth speaketh deceit, and their right hand is a right hand of falsehood.

I will sing a new song unto thee, O God:
Upon a psaltery of ten strings will I sing praises unto thee.

It is he that giveth salvation unto kings:
Who rescueth David his servant from the hurtful sword.

Rescue me, and deliver me out of the hand of aliens,
Whose mouth speaketh vanity, and their right hand is a right hand of falsehood.

When our sons shall be as plants grown up in their youth;
And our daughters as corner stones hewn after the fashion of a palace;

When our garners are full, affording all manner of store;
And our sheep bring forth thousands and ten thousands in our fields:

When our oxen are well laden; when there is no breaking in, and no going forth,
And no outcry in our streets;

Happy is the people, that is in such a case:
Yea, happy is the people, whose God is the Lord.

Ps. 147. PRAISE ye the Lord; for it is good to sing praises unto our God;
For it is pleasant, and praise is comely.

The Lord doth build up Jerusalem;
He gathereth together the outcasts of Israel.

He healeth the broken in heart,
And bindeth up their wounds.

He telleth the number of the stars;
He giveth them all their names.

GOD'S GLORY IN PROVIDENCE AND GRACE.

Great is our Lord, and mighty in power;
His understanding is infinite.
The Lord upholdeth the meek:
He bringeth the wicked down to the ground.
Sing unto the Lord with thanksgiving;
Sing praises upon the harp unto our God:
Who covereth the heaven with clouds,
Who prepareth rain for the earth,
Who maketh grass to grow upon the mountains.
He giveth to the beast his food, and to the young ravens which cry.
He delighteth not in the strength of the horse:
He taketh no pleasure in the legs of a man.
The Lord taketh pleasure in them that fear him,
In those that hope in his mercy.
Praise the Lord, O Jerusalem;
Praise thy God, O Zion.
For he hath strengthened the bars of thy gates;
He hath blessed thy children within thee.
He maketh peace in thy borders;
He filleth thee with the finest of the wheat.
He sendeth out his commandment upon earth;
His word runneth very swiftly.
He giveth snow like wool;
He scattereth the hoar frost like ashes.
He casteth forth his ice like morsels:
Who can stand before his cold?
He sendeth out his word, and melteth them:
He causeth his wind to blow, and the waters flow.
He sheweth his word unto Jacob, his statutes and his judgment unto Israel.
He hath not dealt so with any nation:
As for his judgments, they have not known them.
Praise ye the Lord.

THIRTY-SEVENTH LESSON.

Ps. 39. I SAID, I will take heed to my ways,
That I sin not with my tongue:
I will keep my mouth with a bridle,
While the wicked is before me.
I was dumb with silence, I held my peace, even from good;
And my sorrow was stirred.
My heart was hot within me;
While I was musing the fire kindled:
Then spake I with my tongue:
Lord, make me to know mine end,
And the measure of my days, what it is;
Let me know how frail I am.
Behold, thou hast made my days *as* handbreadths; and mine age is as nothing before thee:
Surely every man at his best estate is altogether vanity.
Surely every man walketh in a vain shew: surely they are disquieted in vain:
He heapeth up riches, and knoweth not who shall gather them.
And now, Lord, what wait I for?
My hope is in thee.
Deliver me from all my transgressions:
Make me not the reproach of the foolish.
I was dumb, I opened not my mouth;
Because thou didst it.
Remove thy stroke away from me:
I am consumed by the blow of thine hand.
When thou with rebukes dost correct man for iniquity, thou makest his beauty to consume away like a moth:
Surely every man is vanity.
Hear my prayer, O Lord, and give ear unto my cry;
Hold not thy peace at my tears:
For I am a stranger with thee,
A sojourner, as all my fathers were.
O spare me, that I may recover strength,
Before I go hence, and be no more.

HUMAN FRAILTY

Job 7: 1-10. Is there not a warfare to man upon earth?
  And are not his days like the days of an hireling?
As a servant that earnestly desireth the shadow,
  And as an hireling that looketh for his wages:
So am I made to possess months of vanity,
  And wearisome nights are appointed to me.
When I lie down, I say, When shall I arise, and the night be gone?
  And I am full of tossings to and fro unto the dawning of the day.
My flesh is clothed with worms and clods of dust;
  My skin closeth up and breaketh out afresh.
My days are swifter than a weaver's shuttle,
  And are spent without hope.
Oh remember that my life is a breath;
  Mine eye shall no more see good.
The eye of him that seeth me shall behold me no more:
  Thine eyes shall be upon me, but I shall not be.
As the cloud is consumed and vanisheth away,
  So he that goeth down to Sheol shall come up no more.
He shall return no more to his house,
  Neither shall his place know him any more.

THIRTY-EIGHTH LESSON.

Ps. 90. LORD, thou hast been our dwelling place in all generations.
  Before the mountains were brought forth,
Or ever thou hadst formed the earth and the world,
  Even from everlasting to everlasting, thou art God.
Thou turnest man to destruction;
  And sayest, Return, ye children of men.
For a thousand years in thy sight are but as yesterday when it is past,
  And as a watch in the night.
Thou carriest them away as with a flood; they are as a sleep:
  In the morning they are like grass which groweth up.
In the morning it flourisheth, and groweth up;
  In the evening it is cut down, and withereth.

HUMAN FRAILTY.

For we are consumed in thine anger,
And in thy wrath are we troubled.
Thou hast set our iniquities before thee,
Our secret sins in the light of thy countenance.
For all our days are passed away in thy wrath :
We bring our years to an end as a sigh.
The days of our years are threescore years and ten,
Or even by reason of strength fourscore years ;
Yet is their pride but labor and sorrow ;
For it is soon gone, and we fly away.
Who knoweth the power of thine anger,
And thy wrath according to the fear that is due unto thee?
So teach us to number our days,
That we may get us an heart of wisdom.
Return, O Lord ; how long ?
And let it repent thee concerning thy servants.
O satisfy us in the morning with thy mercy ;
That we may rejoice and be glad all our days.
Make us glad according to the days wherein thou hast afflicted us,
And the years wherein we have seen evil.
Let thy work appear unto thy servants,
And thy glory upon their children.
And let the favor of the Lord our God be upon us : and establish thou the work of our hands upon us ;
Yea, the work of our hands establish thou it.

THIRTY-NINTH LESSON.

JOB 14. Man that is born of a woman
Is of few days, and full of trouble.
He cometh forth like a flower, and is cut down :
He fleeth also as a shadow, and continueth not.
And dost thou open thine eyes upon such an one,
And bringest me into judgment with thee?
Who can bring a clean thing out of an unclean ? not one.
Seeing his days are determined, the number of his months is with thee,

HUMAN FRAILTY.

And thou hast appointed his bounds that he cannot pass;
    Look away from him, that he may rest, till he shall accomplish, as an hireling, his day.
For there is hope of a tree, if it be cut down, that it will sprout again,
    And that the tender branch thereof will not cease.
Though the root thereof wax old in the earth,
    And the stock thereof die in the ground;
Yet through the scent of water it will bud,
    And put forth boughs like a plant.
But man dieth, and is laid low:
    Yea, man giveth up the ghost, and where is he?
As the waters fail from the sea,
    And the river wasteth and drieth up;
So man lieth down and riseth not:
    Till the heavens be no more, they shall not awake, nor be roused out of their sleep.
Oh that thou wouldest hide me in Sheol, that thou wouldest keep me secret, until thy wrath be past,
    That thou wouldest appoint me a set time, and remember me!
If a man die, shall he live *again?*
    All the days of my warfare would I wait, till my release should come.
Thou shouldest call, and I would answer thee:
    Thou wouldest have a desire to the work of thine hands.
But now thou numberest my steps:
    Dost thou not watch over my sin?
My transgression is sealed up in a bag,
    And thou fastenest up mine iniquity.
And surely the mountain falling cometh to nought,
    And the rock is removed out of its place;
The waters wear the stones;
    The overflowings thereof wash away the dust of the earth:
So thou destroyest the hope of man.
    Thou prevailest for ever against him, and he passeth;
Thou changest his countenance, and sendest him away.
    His sons come to honor, and he knoweth it not;
And they are brought low, but he perceiveth it not of them.
    But his flesh upon him hath pain, and his soul within him mourneth.

HUMAN FRAILTY.

FORTIETH LESSON.

Ps. 102. Hear my prayer, O Lord, and let my cry come unto thee.
Hide not thy face from me in the day of my distress;
Incline thine ear unto me;
In the day when I call answer me speedily.
For my days consume away like smoke,
And my bones are burned as a firebrand.
My heart is smitten like grass, and withered;
For I forget to eat my bread.
By reason of the voice of my groaning my bones cleave to my flesh.
I am like a pelican of the wilderness;
I am become as an owl of the waste places.
I watch, and am become like a sparrow that is alone upon the house-top.
Mine enemies reproach me all the day;
They that are mad against me do curse by me.
For I have eaten ashes like bread,
And mingled my drink with weeping.
Because of thine indignation and thy wrath:
For thou hast taken me up, and cast me away.
My days are like a shadow that declineth;
And I am withered like grass.
But thou, O Lord, shalt abide for ever;
And thy memorial name unto all generations.
Thou shalt arise, and have mercy upon Zion:
For it is time to have pity upon her, yea, the set time is come.
For thy servants take pleasure in her stones,
And have pity upon her dust.
So the nations shall fear the name of the Lord,
And all the kings of the earth thy glory:
For the Lord hath built up Zion,
He hath appeared in his glory;
He hath regarded the prayer of the destitute,
And hath not despised their prayer.
This shall be written for the generation to come:
And a people which shall be created shall praise the Lord.

For he hath looked down from the height of his sanctuary;
  From heaven did the Lord behold the earth;
To hear the sighing of the prisoner;
  To loose those that are appointed to death;
That men may declare the name of the Lord in Zion,
  And his praise in Jerusalem;
When the peoples are gathered together,
  And the kingdoms, to serve the Lord.
He weakened my strength in the way;
  He shortened my days.
I said, O my God, take me not away in the midst of my days:
  Thy years are throughout all generations.
Of old hast thou laid the foundation of the earth;
  And the heavens are the work of thy hands.
They shall perish, but thou shalt endure:
  Yea, all of them shall wax old like a garment:
As a vesture shalt thou change them, and they shall be changed:
  But thou art the same, and thy years shall have no end.
The children of thy servants shall continue,
  And their seed shall be established before thee.

FORTY-FIRST LESSON.

Ps. 30. I WILL extol thee, O Lord; for thou has raised me up,
  And hast not made my foes to rejoice over me.
O Lord my God,
  I cried unto thee, and thou hast healed me.
O Lord, thou hast brought up my soul from Sheol:
  Thou hast kept me alive, that I should not go down to the pit.
Sing praise unto the Lord, O ye saints of his,
  And give thanks to his memorial name.
For his anger is but for a moment;
  His favor is for a life time:
Weeping may tarry for the night,
  But joy cometh in the morning.

As for me, I said in my prosperity,
   I shall never be moved.

Thou, Lord, of thy favor hadst made my mountain to stand strong:
   Thou didst hide thy face; I was troubled.

I cried to thee, O Lord;
   And unto the Lord I made supplication:

What profit is there in my blood, when I go down to the pit?
   Shall the dust praise thee? shall it declare thy truth?

Hear, O Lord, and have mercy upon me:
   Lord, be thou my helper.

Thou hast turned for me my mourning into dancing;
   Thou hast loosed my sackcloth, and girded me with gladness:

To the end that *my* glory may sing praise to thee, and not be silent.
   O Lord my God, I will give thanks unto thee for ever.

Ps. 62.   My soul waiteth in silence for God only:
   From him cometh my salvation.

He only is my rock and my salvation:
   He is my high tower; I shall not be greatly moved.

How long will ye set upon a man,
   That ye may slay him, all of you,

Like a leaning wall, like a tottering fence? they only consult to thrust him down from his dignity; they delight in lies:
   They bless with their mouth, but they curse inwardly.

My soul, wait thou in silence for God only;
   For my expectation is from him.

He only is my rock and my salvation:
   He is my high tower; I shall not be moved.

With God is my salvation and my glory:
   The rock of my strength, and my refuge, is in God.

Trust in him at all times, ye people; pour out your heart before him:
   God is a refuge for us.

Surely men of low degree are vanity, and men of high degree are a lie:
   In the balances they will go up; they are together lighter than vanity.

Trust not in oppression, and become not vain in robbery:
   If riches increase, set not your heart thereon.

God hath spoken once, twice have I heard this;
   That power belongeth unto God:

Also unto thee, O Lord, belongeth mercy:
   For thou renderest to every man according to his work.

FORTY-SECOND LESSON.

Ps. 28. Unto thee, O Lord, will I call;
   My rock, be not thou deaf unto me:

Lest, if thou be silent unto me,
   I become like them that go down into the pit.

Hear the voice of my supplications, when I cry unto thee,
   When I lift up my hands toward thy holy oracle.

Draw me not away with the wicked,
   And with the workers of iniquity:

Which speak peace with their neighbors,
   But mischief is in their hearts.

Give them according to their work, and according to the wickedness of their doings:
   Give them after the operation of their hands;

Render to them their desert.
   Because they regard not the works of the Lord,

Nor the operation of his hands,
   He shall break them down and not build them up.

Blessed be the Lord,
   Because he hath heard the voice of my supplications.

The Lord is my strength and my shield;
   My heart hath trusted in him, and I am helped:

Therefore my heart greatly rejoiceth;
   And with my song will I praise him.

The Lord is their strength,
   And he is a strong hold of salvation to his anointed.

Save thy people, and bless thine inheritance:
   Be their shepherd also, and bear them up for ever.

MAN'S REFUGE IN GOD.

Ps. 20. The Lord answer thee in the day of trouble;
    The name of the God of Jacob set thee up on high;
Send thee help from the sanctuary,
    And strengthen thee out of Zion:
Remember all thy offerings,
    And accept thy burnt sacrifice;
Grant thee thy heart's desire,
    And fulfil all thy counsel.
We will triumph in thy salvation,
    And in the name of our God we will set up our banners:
The Lord fulfil all thy petitions.
    Now know I that the Lord saveth his anointed;
He will answer him from his holy heaven
    With the saving strength of his right hand.
Some *trust* in chariots, and some in horses:
    But we will make mention of the name of the Lord our God.
They are bowed down and fallen:
    But we are risen, and stand upright.
Save, Lord:
    Let the King answer us when we call.

Ps. 124. If it had not been the Lord who was on our side,
    Let Israel now say;
If it had not been the Lord who was on our side,
    When men rose up against us:
Then they had swallowed us up alive,
    When their wrath was kindled against us:
Then the waters had overwhelmed us, the stream had gone over our soul:
    Then the proud waters had gone over our soul.
Blessed be the Lord,
    Who hath not given us as a prey to their teeth.
Our soul is escaped as a bird out of the snare of the fowlers:
    The snare is broken, and we are escaped.
Our help is in the name of the Lord,
    Who made heaven and earth.

FORTY-THIRD LESSON

Ps. 13. How long, O Lord, wilt thou forget me for ever?
How long wilt thou hide thy face from me?
How long shall I take counsel in my soul, having sorrow in my heart all the day?
How long shall mine enemy be exalted over me?
Consider *and* answer me, O Lord my God;
Lighten mine eyes, lest I sleep the sleep of death;
Lest mine enemy say, I have prevailed against him;
Lest mine adversaries rejoice when I am moved.
But I have trusted in thy mercy; my heart shall rejoice in thy salvation:
I will sing unto the Lord, because he hath dealt bountifully with me.

Ps. 123. Unto thee do I lift up mine eyes,
O thou that sittest in the heavens.
Behold, as the eyes of servants *look* unto the hand of their master,
As the eyes of a maiden unto the hand of her mistress;
So our eyes *look* unto the Lord our God,
Until he have mercy upon us.
Have mercy upon us, O Lord, have mercy upon us:
For we are exceedingly filled with contempt.
Our soul is exceedingly filled with the scorning of those that are at ease,
And with the contempt of the proud.

Ps. 17. Hear the right, O Lord, attend unto my cry;
Give ear unto my prayer, that goeth not out of feigned lips.
Let my sentence come forth from thy presence;
Let thine eyes look upon equity.
Thou hast proved mine heart; thou hast visited me in the night;
Thou hast tried me, and findest nothing;
I am purposed that my mouth shall not transgress.
As for the works of men, by the word of thy lips I have kept me from the ways of the violent.
My steps have held fast to thy paths,
My feet have not slipped.

I have called upon thee, for thou wilt answer me, O God :
Incline thine ear unto me, and hear my speech.

Shew thy marvellous loving-kindness, O thou that savest by thy right hand them which put their trust *in thee,*
From those that rise up against them, by thy right hand.

Keep me as the apple of the eye,
Hide me under the shadow of thy wings,

From the wicked that oppress me,
My deadly enemies, that compass me about.

From men of the world, whose portion is in *this* life,
And whose belly thou fillest with thy treasure:

They are satisfied with children,
And leave the rest of their substance to their babes.

As for me, I shall behold thy face in righteousness :
I shall be satisfied, when I awake, with beholding thy form.

FORTY-FOURTH LESSON.

Ps. 27. The Lord is my light and my salvation ; whom shall I fear?
The Lord is the strength of my life ; of whom shall I be afraid?

When evil-doers came upon me to eat up my flesh,
Even mine adversaries and my foes, they stumbled and fell.

Though an host should encamp against me,
My heart shall not fear:

Though war should rise against me,
Even then will I be confident.

One thing have I asked of the Lord, that will I seek after ;
That I may dwell in the house of the Lord all the days of my life,

To behold the beauty of the Lord, and to inquire in his temple.
For in the day of trouble he shall keep me secretly in his pavilion:

In the covert of his tabernacle shall he hide me ; he shall lift me up upon a rock.
And now shall mine head be lifted up above mine enemies round about me;

And I will offer in his tabernacle sacrifices of joy ;
I will sing, yea, I will sing praises unto the Lord.

Hear, O Lord, when I cry with my voice:
Have mercy also upon me, and answer me.
When thou saidst, Seek ye my face; my heart said unto thee,
Thy face, Lord, will I seek.
Hide not thy face from me;
Put not thy servant away in anger:
Thou hast been my help;
Cast me not off, neither forsake me, O God of my salvation.
For my father and my mother have forsaken me,
But the Lord will take me up.
Teach me thy way, O Lord;
And lead me in a plain path, because of mine enemies.
Deliver me not over unto the will of mine adversaries:
For false witnesses are risen up against me, and such as breathe out cruelty.
I had fainted, unless I had believed to see the goodness of the Lord in the land of the living.
Wait on the Lord;
Be strong, and let thine heart take courage;
Yea, wait thou on the Lord.

Ps. 61. HEAR my cry, O God;
Attend unto my prayer.
From the end of the earth will I call unto thee, when my heart is overwhelmed:
Lead me to the rock that is higher than I.
For thou hast been a refuge for me,
A strong tower from the enemy.
I will dwell in thy tabernacle for ever:
I will take refuge in the covert of thy wings.
For thou, O God, hast heard my vows:
Thou hast given me the heritage of those that fear thy name.
Thou wilt prolong the king's life:
His years shall be as many generations.
He shall abide before God for ever:
O prepare loving-kindness and truth, that they may preserve him.
So will I sing praise unto thy name for ever,
That I may daily perform my vows.

FORTY-FIFTH LESSON.

Ps. 71. IN thee, O Lord, do I put my trust:
    Let me never be ashamed.
Deliver me in thy righteousness, and rescue me:
    Bow down thine ear unto me, and save me.
Be thou to me a rock of habitation, whereunto I may continually resort:
    Thou hast given commandment to save me; for thou art my rock and my fortress.
Rescue me, O my God, out of the hand of the wicked,
    Out of the hand of the unrighteous and cruel man.
For thou art my hope, O Lord God:
    Thou art my trust from my youth.
By thee have I been holden up from the womb:
    Thou art he that took me out of my mother's bowels:
My praise shall be continually of thee.
    I am as a wonder unto many; but thou art my strong refuge.
My mouth shall be filled with thy praise,
    And with thy honor all the day.
Cast me not off in the time of old age;
    Forsake me not when my strength faileth.
For mine enemies speak concerning me;
    And they that watch for my soul take counsel together,
Saying, God hath forsaken him:
    Pursue and take him; for there is none to deliver.
O God, be not far from me:
    O my God, make haste to help me.
Let them be ashamed *and* consumed that are adversaries to my soul;
    Let them be covered with reproach and dishonor that seek my hurt.
But I will hope continually,
    And will praise thee yet more and more.
My mouth shall tell of thy righteousness, *and* of thy salvation all the day;
    For I know not the numbers thereof.
I will come with the mighty acts of the Lord God:
    I will make mention of thy righteousness, even of thine only.
O God, thou hast taught me from my youth;
    And hitherto have I declared thy wondrous works.

Yea, even when I am old and grayheaded, O God, forsake me not;
    Until I have declared thy strength unto the next generation,

Thy might to every one that is to come.
    Thy righteousness also, O God, is very high;

Thou who hast done great things,
    O God, who is like unto thee?

Thou, which hast shewed us many and sore troubles, shalt quicken us again,
    And shalt bring us up again from the depths of the earth.

Increase thou my greatness,
    And turn again and comfort me.

I will also praise thee with the psaltery,
    Even thy truth, O my God:

Unto thee will I sing praises with the harp,
    O thou Holy One of Israel.

My lips shall greatly rejoice when I sing praises unto thee
    And my soul, which thou hast redeemed.

My tongue also shall talk of thy righteousness all the day long·
    For they are ashamed, for they are confounded, that seek my hurt.

FORTY-SIXTH LESSON.

Ps. 3. LORD, how are mine adversaries increased!
    Many are they that rise up against me

Many there be which say of my soul,
    There is no help for him in God.

But thou, O Lord, art a shield about me;
    My glory, and the lifter up of mine head.

I cry unto the Lord with my voice,
    And he answereth me out of his holy hill.

I laid me down and slept;
    I awaked; for the Lord sustaineth me.

I will not be afraid of ten thousands of the people,
    That have set themselves against me round about.

Arise, O Lord: save me, O my God: for thou hast smitten all mine enemies upon the cheek bone;
Thou hast broken the teeth of the wicked.
Salvation belongeth unto the Lord:
Thy blessing be upon thy people.

Ps. 86. Bow down thine ear, O Lord, and answer me;
For I am poor and needy.
Preserve my soul; for I am godly:
O thou my God, save thy servant that trusteth in thee.
Be merciful unto me, O Lord;
For unto thee do I cry all the day long.
Rejoice the soul of thy servant;
For unto thee, O Lord, do I lift up my soul.
For thou, Lord, art good, and ready to forgive,
And plenteous in mercy unto all them that call upon thee.
Give ear, O Lord, unto my prayer;
And hearken unto the voice of my supplications.
In the day of my trouble I will call upon thee;
For thou wilt answer me.
There is none like unto thee among the gods, O Lord;
Neither are there any works like unto thy works.
All nations whom thou hast made shall come and worship before thee, O Lord;
And they shall glorify thy name.
For thou art great, and doest wondrous things:
Thou art God alone.
Teach me thy way, O Lord; I will walk in thy truth:
Unite my heart to fear thy name.
I will praise thee, O Lord my God, with my whole heart;
And I will glorify thy name for evermore.
For great is thy mercy toward me;
And thou hast delivered my soul from the lowest pit.
O God, the proud are risen up against me, and the congregation of violent men have sought after my soul,
And have not set thee before them.

But thou, O Lord, art a God full of compassion and gracious,
Slow to anger, and plenteous in mercy and truth.

O turn unto me, and have mercy upon me;
Give thy strength unto thy servant,

And save the son of thine handmaid.
Shew me a token for good;

That they which hate me may see it, and be ashamed,
Because thou, Lord, has holpen me, and comforted me.

FORTY-SEVENTH LESSON.

Ps. 46. God is our refuge and strength,
A very present help in trouble.

Therefore will we not fear, though the earth do change,
And though the mountains be moved in the heart of the seas;

Though the waters thereof roar and be troubled,
Though the mountains shake with the swelling thereof.

There is a river, the streams whereof make glad the city of God,
The holy place of the tabernacles of the Most High.

God is in the midst of her; she shall not be moved:
God shall help her, and that right early.

The nations raged, the kingdoms were moved:
He uttered his voice, the earth melted.

The Lord of hosts is with us;
The God of Jacob is our refuge.

Come, behold the works of the Lord, what desolations he hath made in the earth.
He maketh wars to cease unto the end of the earth;

He breaketh the bow, and cutteth the spear in sunder;
He burneth the chariots in the fire.

Be still, and know that I am God:
I will be exalted among the nations, I will be exalted in the earth.

The Lord of hosts is with us:
The God of Jacob is our refuge.

MAN'S REFUGE IN GOD.

Ps. 115. Not unto us, O Lord, not unto us, but unto thy name give glory,
 For thy mercy, and for thy truth's sake.
Wherefore should the nations say,
 Where is now their God?
But our God is in the heavens:
 He hath done whatsoever he pleased.
Their idols are silver and gold,
 The work of men's hands.
They have mouths, but they speak not;
 Eyes have they, but they see not:
They have ears, but they hear not;
 Noses have they, but they smell not:
They have hands, but they handle not: feet have they, but they walk not;
 Neither speak they through their throat.
They that make them shall be like unto them;
 Yea, every one that trusteth in them.
O Israel, trust thou in the Lord:
 He is their help and their shield.
O house of Aaron, trust ye in the Lord:
 He is their help and their shield.
Ye that fear the Lord, trust in the Lord:
 He is their help and their shield.
The Lord has been mindful of us; he will bless us:
 He will bless the house of Israel; he will bless the house of Aaron.
He will bless them that fear the Lord,
 Both small and great.
The Lord increase you more and more,
 You and your children.
Blessed are ye of the Lord,
 Which made heaven and earth.
The heavens are the heavens of the Lord;
 But the earth hath he given to the children of men.
The dead praise not the Lord,
 Neither any that go down into silence:
But we will bless the Lord from this time forth and for evermore.
 Praise ye the Lord.

MAN'S REFUGE IN GOD.

FORTY-EIGHTH LESSON.

Ps. 41. BLESSED is he that considereth the poor:.
The Lord will deliver him in the day of evil.
The Lord will preserve him, and keep him alive, and he shall be blessed upon the earth;
And deliver not thou him unto the will of his enemies.
The Lord will support him upon the couch of languishing.
Thou makest all his bed in his sickness.
I said, O Lord, have mercy upon me:
Heal my soul; for I have sinned against thee.
Mine enemies speak evil against me, *saying*,
When shall he die, and his name perish?
And if he come to see *me*, he speaketh falsehood; his heart gathereth iniquity to itself:
When he goeth abroad, he telleth it.
All that hate me whisper together against me:
Against me do they devise my hurt.
An evil disease, *say they*, cleaveth fast unto him:
And now that he lieth he shall rise up no more.
Yea, mine own familiar friend, in whom I trusted, which did eat of my bread,
Hath lifted up his heel against me.
But thou, O Lord, have mercy upon me, and raise me up,
That I may requite them.
By this I know that thou delightest in me,
Because mine enemy doth not triumph over me.
And as for me, thou upholdest me in mine integrity,
And settest me before thy face for ever.
Blessed be the Lord, the God of Israel,
From everlasting and to everlasting. Amen, and Amen.

Ps. 44. WE have heard with our ears, O God, our fathers have told us,
What work thou didst in their days, in the days of old.
Thou didst drive out the nations with thy hand, but them thou didst plant;
Thou didst afflict the peoples, but them thou didst spread abroad.
For they gat not the land in possession by their own sword,
Neither did their own arm save them:

MAN'S REFUGE IN GOD.

But thy right hand, and thine arm, and the light of thy countenance,
Because thou hadst a favor unto them.

Thou art my King, O God:
Command deliverance for Jacob.

Through thee will we push down our adversaries:
Through thy name will we tread them under that rise up against us.

For I will not trust in my bow,
Neither shall my sword save me.

But thou hast saved us from our adversaries,
And hast put them to shame that hate us.

In God have we made our boast all the day long,
And we will give thanks unto thy name for ever.

FORTY-NINTH LESSON.

Ps. 142. I CRY with my voice unto the Lord;
With my voice unto the Lord do I make supplication.

I pour out my complaint before him;
I shew before him my trouble.

When my spirit was overwhelmed within me, thou knewest my path.
In the way wherein I walk have they hidden a snare for me.

Look on my right hand, and see; for there is no man that knoweth me:
Refuge hath failed me; no man careth for my soul.

I cried unto thee, O Lord;
I said, Thou art my refuge, my portion in the land of the living.

Attend unto my cry; for I am brought very low:
Deliver me from my persecutors; for they are stronger than I.

Bring my soul out of prison, that I may give thanks unto thy name:
The righteous shall compass me about; for thou shalt deal bountifully with me.

Ps. 143. HEAR my prayer, O Lord; give ear to my supplications:
In thy faithfulness answer me, and in thy righteousness.

And enter not into judgment with thy servant;
For in thy sight no man living is righteous.

For the enemy hath persecuted my soul; he hath smitten my life down
  to the ground:
  He hath made me to dwell in dark places, as those that have been long dead
Therefore is my spirit overwhelmed within me;
  My heart within me is desolate.
I remember the days of old; I meditate on all thy doings:
  I muse on the work of thy hands.
I spread forth my hands unto thee:
  My soul thirsteth after thee, as a weary land.
Make haste to answer me, O Lord; my spirit faileth:
  Hide not thy face from me; lest I become like them that go down into the pit.
Cause me to hear thy loving-kindness in the morning;
  For in thee do I trust:
Cause me to know the way wherein I should walk;
  For I lift up my soul unto thee.
Deliver me, O Lord, from mine enemies:
  I flee unto thee to hide me.
Teach me to do thy will; for thou art my God:
  Thy spirit is good; lead me in the land of uprightness.
Quicken me, O Lord, for thy name's sake:
  In thy righteousness bring my soul out of trouble.
And in thy loving-kindness cut off mine enemies, and destroy all them
  that afflict my soul;
  For I am thy servant.

Ps. 73: 25-28. Whom have I in heaven *but thee?*
  And there is none upon earth that I desire beside thee.
My flesh and my heart faileth:
  But God is the strength of my heart and my portion for ever.
For, lo, they that are *departing* from thee shall perish ·
  But it is good for me to draw near unto God:
I have made the Lord God my refuge,
  That I may tell of all thy works.

MAN'S REFUGE IN GOD.

FIFTIETH LESSON.

Ps. 56. Be merciful unto me, O God; for man would swallow me up:
All the day long he fighting oppresseth me.
Mine enemies would swallow me up all the day long:
For they be many that fight proudly against me.
What time I am afraid, I will put my trust in thee.
In God (I will praise his word,)
In God have I put my trust, I will not be afraid;
What can flesh do unto me?
All the day long they wrest my words:
All their thoughts are against me for evil.
They gather themselves together, they hide themselves, they mark my steps,
Even as they have waited for my soul.
Shall they escape by iniquity?
In anger cast down the peoples, O God.
Thou tellest my wanderings: put thou my tears into thy bottle;
Are they not in thy book?
Then shall mine enemies turn back in the day that I call:
This I know, that God is for me.
In God (I will praise his word,)
In Jehovah (I will praise his word,)
In God have I put my trust, I will not be afraid;
What can man do unto me?
Thy vows are upon me, O God: I will render thank offerings unto thee.
For thou hast delivered my soul from death.
Hast thou not *delivered* my feet from falling?
That I may walk before God in the light of the living.

Ps. 81. Sing aloud unto God our strength:
Make a joyful noise unto the God of Jacob.
Take up the psalm, and bring hither the timbrel,
The pleasant harp with the psaltery.
Blow up the trumpet in the new moon,
At the full moon, on our solemn feast day.
For it is a statute for Israel,
An ordinance of the God of Jacob.

He appointed it in Joseph for a testimony, when he went out over the land of Egypt:
Where I heard a language that I knew not.

I removed his shoulder from the burden:
His hands were freed from the basket.

Thou calledst in trouble, and I delivered thee; I answered thee in the secret place of thunder;
I proved thee at the waters of Meribah.

Hear, O my people, and I will testify unto thee:
O Israel, if thou wouldest hearken unto me!

There shall no strange god be in thee;
Neither shalt thou worship any strange god.

I am the Lord thy God, which brought thee up out of the land of Egypt:
Open thy mouth wide, and I will fill it.

But my people hearkened not to my voice;
And Israel would none of me.

So I let them go after the stubbornness of their heart,
That they might walk in their own counsels.

Oh that my people would hearken unto me,
That Israel would walk in my ways!

I should soon subdue their enemies,
And turn my hand against their adversaries.

The haters of the Lord should submit themselves unto him:
But their time should endure for ever.

He should feed them also with the finest of the wheat:
And with honey out of the rock should I satisfy thee.

FIFTY-FIRST LESSON.

Ps. 37. FRET not thyself because of evil-doers,
Neither be thou envious against them that work unrighteousness.

For they shall soon be cut down like the grass,
And wither as the green herb.

Trust in the Lord, and do good;
Dwell in the land, and feed on his faithfulness.

MAN'S REFUGE IN GOD.

Delight thyself also in the Lord;
    And he shall give thee the desires of thine heart.
Commit thy way unto the Lord;
    Trust also in him, and he shall bring it to pass.
And he shall make thy righteousness to go forth as the light,
    And thy judgment as the noonday.
Rest in the Lord, and wait patiently for him: fret not thyself because of him who prospereth in his way,
    Because of the man who bringeth wicked devices to pass.
Cease from anger, and escape wrath:
    Fret not thyself, it tendeth only to evil-doing.
For evil-doers shall be cut off:
    But those that wait upon the Lord, they shall inherit the land.
For yet a little while, and the wicked shall not be:
    Yea, thou shalt diligently consider his place, and he shall not be.
But the meek shall inherit the land;
    And shall delight themselves in the abundance of peace.
A man's goings are established of the Lord;
    And he delighteth in his way.
Though he fall, he shall not be utterly cast down:
    For the Lord upholdeth him with his hand.
I have been young, and now am old;
    Yet have I not seen the righteous forsaken, nor his seed begging their bread.
All the day long he dealeth graciously, and lendeth;
    And his seed is blessed.
Depart from evil, and do good;
    And dwell for evermore.
For the Lord loveth judgment, and forsaketh not his saints;
    They are preserved for ever:
But the seed of the wicked shall be cut off.
    The righteous shall inherit the land, and dwell therein for ever.
The mouth of the righteous talketh of wisdom,
    And his tongue speaketh judgment.
The law of his God is in his heart;
    None of his steps shall slide.

The wicked watcheth the righteous, and seeketh to slay him.
The Lord will not leave him in his hand, nor condemn him when he is judged.
Wait on the Lord, and keep his way, and he shall exalt thee to inherit the land:
When the wicked are cut off, thou shalt see it.
I have seen the wicked in great power,
And spreading himself like a green tree in its native soil.
But one passed by, and, lo, he was not:
Yea, I sought him, but he could not be found.
Mark the perfect man, and behold the upright:
For their is a happy end to the man of peace.
As for transgressors, they shall be destroyed together:
The end of the wicked shall be cut off.
But the salvation of the righteous is of the Lord:
He is their strong hold in the time of trouble.
And the Lord helpeth them, and rescueth them:
He rescueth them from the wicked, and saveth them, because they have taken refuge in him.

FIFTY-SECOND LESSON.

Ps. 88. O Lord, the God of my salvation,
I have cried day and night before thee:
Let my prayer enter into thy presence;
Incline thine ear unto my cry:
For my soul is full of troubles,
And my life draweth nigh unto Sheol.
I am counted with them that go down into the pit;
I am as a man that hath no help:
Cast off among the dead,
Like the slain that lie in the grave,
Whom thou rememberest no more;
And they are cut off from thy hand.
Thou hast laid me in the lowest pit,
In dark places, in the deeps.

Thy wrath lieth hard upon me,
  And thou hast afflicted me with all thy waves.
Thou hast put mine acquaintance far from me;
  Thou hast made me an abomination unto them:
I am shut up, and I cannot come forth.
  Mine eye wasteth away by reason of affliction:
I have called daily upon thee, O Lord,
  I have spread forth my hands unto thee.
Wilt thou shew wonders to the dead?
  Shall they that are deceased arise and praise thee?
Shall thy loving-kindness be declared in the grave?
  Or thy faithfulness in Destruction?
Shall thy wonders be known in the dark?
  And thy righteousness in the land of forgetfulness?
But unto thee, O Lord, have I cried,
  And in the morning shall my prayer come before thee.
Lord, why castest thou off my soul?
  Why hidest thou thy face from me?
I am afflicted and ready to die from my youth up:
  While I suffer thy terrors I am distracted.
Thy fierce wrath is gone over me;
  Thy terrors have cut me off.
They came round about me like water all the day long;
  They compassed me about together.
Lover and friend hast thou put far from me,
  And mine acquaintance into darkness.

Ps. 4. Answer me when I call, O God of my righteousness; thou hast set me at large *when I was* in distress:
  Have mercy upon me, and hear my prayer.
O ye sons of men, how long shall my glory be turned into dishonor?
  How long will ye love vanity, and seek after falsehood?
But know that the Lord hath set apart him that is godly for himself:
  The Lord will hear when I call unto him.
Stand in awe, and sin not:
  Commune with your own heart upon your bed, and be still.

Offer the sacrifices of righteousness,
    And put your trust in the Lord.

Many there be that say, Who will shew us *any* good?
    Lord, lift thou up the light of thy countenance upon us.

Thou hast put gladness in my heart,
    More than they have when their corn and their wine are increased.

In peace will I both lay me down and sleep:
    For thou, Lord, alone makest me dwell in safety.

FIFTY-THIRD LESSON.

DEUT. 32. GIVE ear, ye heavens, and I will speak;
    And let the earth hear the words of my mouth:

My doctrine shall drop as the rain,
    My speech shall distil as the dew;

As the small rain upon the tender grass,
    And as the showers upon the herb:

For I will proclaim the name of the Lord:
    Ascribe ye greatness unto our God.

The Rock, his work is perfect;
    For all his ways are judgment:

A God of faithfulness and without iniquity,
    Just and right is he.

They have dealt corruptly with him, *they are* not his children, *it is* their blemish;
    They are a perverse and crooked generation.

Do ye thus requite the Lord,
    O foolish people and unwise?

Is not he thy father that hath bought thee?
    He hath made thee, and established thee.

Remember the days of old,
    Consider the years of many generations:

Ask thy father, and he will shew thee;
    Thine elders, and they will tell thee.

MAN'S REFUGE IN GOD.

When the Most High gave to the nations their inheritance,
    When he separated the children of men,
He set the bounds of the peoples
    According to the number of the children of Israel.
For the Lord's portion is his people;
    Jacob is the lot of his inheritance.
He found him in a desert land,
    And in the waste howling wilderness;
He compassed him about, he cared for him,
    He kept him as the apple of his eye:
As an eagle that stirreth up her nest,
    That fluttereth over her young,
He spread abroad his wings, he took them,
    He bare them on his pinions:
The Lord alone did lead him,
    And there was no strange god with him.
He made him ride on the high places of the earth,
    And he did eat the increase of the field;
And he made him to suck honey out of the rock,
    And oil out of the flinty rock;
Butter of kine, and milk of sheep,
    With fat of lambs.
Then he forsook God which made him,
    And lightly esteemed the Rock of his salvation.
They have moved me to jealousy with that which is not God;
    They have provoked me to anger with their vanities:
And I will move them to jealousy with those which are not a people;
    I will provoke them to anger with a foolish nation.
Oh that they were wise, that they understood this,
    That they would consider their latter end!
How should one chase a thousand,
    And two put ten thousand to flight,
Except their Rock had sold them,
    And the Lord had delivered them up?
For their rock is not as our Rock,
    Even our enemies themselves being judges.

FIFTY-FOURTH LESSON.

Ps. 26.   Judge me, O Lord, for I have walked in mine integrity:
I have trusted also in the Lord without wavering.

Examine me, O Lord, and prove me;
Try my reins and my heart.

For thy loving-kindness is before mine eyes;
And I have walked in thy truth.

I have not sat with men of falsehood;
Neither will I go in with dissemblers.

I hate the congregation of evil-doers,
And will not sit with the wicked.

I will wash mine hands in innocency;
So will I compass thine altar, O Lord:

That I may make the voice of thanksgiving to be heard,
And tell of all thy wondrous works.

Lord, I love the habitation of thy house,
And the place where thy glory dwelleth.

Gather not my soul with sinners,
Nor my life with men of blood:

In whose hands is mischief,
And their right hand is full of bribes.

But as for me, I will walk in mine integrity:
Redeem me, and be merciful unto me.

My foot standeth in an even place:
In the congregations will I bless the Lord.

Ps. 57.   Be merciful unto me, O God, be merciful unto me;
For my soul taketh refuge in thee:

Yea, in the shadow of thy wings will I take refuge,
Until these calamities be overpast.

I will cry unto God Most High;
Unto God that performeth all things for me.

He shall send from heaven, and save me, *when* he that would swallow me up reproacheth;
God shall send forth his mercy and his truth.

My soul is among lions;
 I lie among them that are set on fire,
Even the sons of men, whose teeth are spears and arrows,
 And their tongue a sharp sword.
Be thou exalted, O God, above the heavens;
 Let thy glory be above all the earth.
They have prepared a net for my steps;
 My soul is bowed down:
They have digged a pit before me;
 They are fallen into the midst thereof themselves.
My heart is fixed, O God, my heart is fixed:
 I will sing, yea, I will sing praises.
Awake up, my glory; awake, psaltery and harp:
 I myself will awake right early.
I will give thanks unto thee, O Lord, among the peoples:
 I will sing praises unto thee among the nations.
For thy mercy is great unto the heavens,
 And thy truth unto the skies.
Be thou exalted, O God, above the heavens;
 Let thy glory be above all the earth.

FIFTY-FIFTH LESSON.

Ps. 7. O Lord my God, in thee do I put my trust:
 Save me from all them that pursue me, and deliver me:
Lest he tear my soul like a lion,
 Rending it in pieces, while there is none to deliver.
O Lord my God, if I have done this;
 If there be iniquity in my hands;
If I have rewarded evil unto him that was at peace with me;
 (Yea, I have delivered him that without cause was mine adversary:)
Let the enemy pursue my soul, and overtake it;
 Yea, let him tread my life down to the earth, and lay my glory in the dust.
Arise, O Lord, in thine anger, lift up thyself against the rage of mine adversaries:
 And awake for me, thou hast commanded judgment.

And let the congregation of the peoples compass thee about:
   And over them return thou on high.
The Lord ministereth judgment to the peoples:
   Judge me, O Lord, according to my righteousness, and to mine integrity that is in me.
Oh let the wickedness of the wicked come to an end, but establish thou the righteous:
   For the righteous God trieth the hearts and reins.
My shield is with God, which saveth the upright in heart.
   God is a righteous judge, yea, a God that hath indignation every day.
If a man turn not, he will whet his sword;
   He hath bent his bow, and made it ready.
He hath also prepared for him the instruments of death;
   He maketh his arrows fiery shafts.
Behold, he travaileth with iniquity;
   Yea, he hath conceived mischief, and brought forth falsehood.
He hath made a pit, and digged it,
   And is fallen into the ditch which he made.
His mischief shall return upon his own head,
   And his violence shall come down upon his own pate.
I will give thanks unto the Lord according to his righteousness:
   And will sing praise to the name of the Lord Most High.

Ps. 54. SAVE me, O God, by thy name, and judge me in thy might.
   Hear my prayer, O God; give ear to the words of my mouth.
For strangers are risen up against me, and violent men have sought after my soul:
   They have not set God before them.
Behold, God is mine helper:
   The Lord is of them that uphold my soul.
He shall requite the evil unto mine enemies:
   Destroy thou them in thy truth.
With a freewill offering will I sacrifice unto thee:
   I will give thanks unto thy name, O Lord, for it is good.
For he hath delivered me out of all trouble;
   And mine eye hath seen my desire upon mine enemies.

GOD OUR DEFENDER AND JUDGE.
FIFTY-SIXTH LESSON.

Ps. 49. Hear this, all ye peoples; give ear, all ye inhabitants of the world:
Both low and high, rich and poor together.

My mouth shall speak wisdom;
And the meditation of my heart shall be of understanding.

I will incline mine ear to a parable:
I will open my dark saying upon the harp.

Wherefore should I fear in the days of evil,
When iniquity at my heels compasseth me about?

They that trust in their wealth, and boast themselves in the multitude of their riches;
None of them can by any means redeem his brother, nor give to God a ransom for him:

(For the redemption of their life is costly, and it faileth for ever:)
That he should still live alway, that he should not see corruption.

For he seeth that wise men die, the fool and the brutish alike perish,
And leave their wealth to others.

Their inward thought is, *that* their houses *shall continue* for ever, *and* their dwelling places to all generations;
They call their lands after their own names.

But man being in honor abideth not:
He is like the beasts that perish.

This their way is their folly:
Yet after them men approve their sayings.

They are appointed as a flock for Sheol;
Death shall be their shepherd:

And the upright shall have dominion over them in the morning;
And their beauty shall be for Sheol to consume, that there be no habitation for it.

But God will redeem my soul from the power of Sheol:
For he shall receive me.

Be not thou afraid when one is made rich,
When the glory of his house is increased:

For when he dieth he shall carry nothing away;
His glory shall not descend after him.

Though while he lived he blessed his soul,
And men praise thee, when thou doest well to thyself,
He shall go to the generation of his fathers; they shall never see the light.
Man that is in honor, and understandeth not, is like the beasts that perish.

Ps. 82. GOD standeth in the congregation of God;
He judgeth among the gods.
How long will ye judge unjustly,
And respect the persons of the wicked?
Judge the poor and fatherless:
Do justice to the afflicted and destitute.
Rescue the poor and needy:
Deliver them out of the hand of the wicked.
They know not, neither do they understand; they walk to and fro in darkness:
All the foundations of the earth are moved.
I said, Ye are gods, and all of you sons of the Most High.
Nevertheless ye shall die like men, and fall like one of the princes.
Arise, O God, judge the earth:
For thou shalt inherit all the nations.

FIFTY-SEVENTH LESSON.

Ps. 94. O LORD, thou God to whom vengeance belongeth,
Thou God to whom vengeance belongeth, shine forth.
Lift up thyself, thou judge of the earth:
Render to the proud their desert.
Lord, how long shall the wicked, how long shall the wicked triumph?
They prate, they speak arrogantly:
All the workers of iniquity boast themselves.
They break in pieces thy people, O Lord, and afflict thine heritage.
They slay the widow and the stranger, and murder the fatherless.
And they say, The Lord shall not see, neither shall the God of Jacob consider.
Consider, ye brutish among the people:
And ye fools, when will ye be wise?
He that planted the ear, shall he not hear?
He that formed the eye, shall he not see?

He that chastiseth the nations, shall not he correct, *even* he that teacheth man knowledge?
  The Lord knoweth the thoughts of man, that they are vanity.
Blessed is the man whom thou chastenest, O Lord,
  And teachest out of thy law:
That thou mayest give him rest from the days of adversity,
  Until the pit be digged for the wicked.
For the Lord will not cast off his people,
  Neither will he forsake his inheritance.
For judgment shall return unto righteousness:
  And all the upright in heart shall follow it.
Who will rise up for me against the evil-doers?
  Who will stand up for me against the workers of iniquity?
Unless the Lord had been my help,
  My soul had soon dwelt in silence.
When I said, My foot slippeth; thy mercy, O Lord, held me up.
  In the multitude of my thoughts within me thy comforts delight my soul.
Shall the throne of wickedness have fellowship with thee,
  Which frameth mischief by statute?
They gather themselves together against the soul of the righteous,
  And condemn the innocent blood.
But the Lord hath been my high tower;
  And my God the rock of my refuge.
And he hath brought upon them their own iniquity, and shall cut them off in their own evil;
  The Lord our God shall cut them off.

Ps. 53. The fool hath said in his heart, There is no God.
  Corrupt are they, and have done abominable iniquity; there is none that doeth good.
God looked down from heaven upon the children of men,
  To see if there were any that did understand, that did seek after God.
Every one of them is gone back; they are together become filthy;
  There is none that doeth good, no, not one.
Have the workers of iniquity no knowledge?
  Who eat up my people as they eat bread, and call not upon God.

There were they in great fear, where no fear was; for God hath scattered the bones of him that encampeth against thee;
Thou hast put them to shame, because God hath rejected them.

Oh that the salvation of Israel were come out of Zion!
When God bringeth back the captivity of his people, then shall Jacob rejoice, and Israel shall be glad.

FIFTY-EIGHTH LESSON.

Ps. 50. GOD, *even* God, the Lord, hath spoken, and called the earth from the rising of the sun unto the going down thereof.
Out of Zion, the perfection of beauty, God hath shined forth.

Our God shall come, and shall not keep silence: a fire shall devour before him,
And it shall be very tempestuous round about him.

He shall call to the heavens above,
And to the earth, that he may judge his people:

Gather my saints together unto me;
Those that have made a covenant with me by sacrifice.

And the heavens shall declare his righteousness;
For God is judge himself.

Hear, O my people, and I will speak; O Israel, and I will testify unto thee:
I am God, even thy God.

I will not reprove thee for thy sacrifices;
And thy burnt offerings are continually before me.

I will take no bullock out of thy house,
Nor he-goats out of thy folds.

For every beast of the forest is mine,
And the cattle upon a thousand hills.

I know all the fowls of the mountains:
And the wild beasts of the field are mine.

If I were hungry, I would not tell thee:
For the world is mine, and the fulness thereof.

Will I eat the flesh of bulls,
Or drink the blood of goats?

Offer unto God the sacrifice of thanksgiving;
And pay thy vows unto the Most High:

And call upon me in the day of trouble;
I will deliver thee, and thou shalt glorify me.

But unto the wicked God saith, What hast thou to do to declare my statutes,
And that thou hast taken my covenant in thy mouth?

Seeing thou hatest instruction,
And castest my words behind thee.

When thou sawest a thief, thou consentedst with him,
And hast been partaker with adulterers.

Thou givest thy mouth to evil,
And thy tongue frameth deceit.

Thou sittest and speakest against thy brother; thou slanderest thine own mother's son.
These things hast thou done, and I kept silence:

Thou thoughtest that I was altogether such an one as thyself;
But I will reprove thee, and set them in order before thine eyes.

Now consider this, ye that forget God,
Lest I tear you in pieces, and there be none to deliver:

Whoso offereth the sacrifice of thanksgiving glorifieth me;
And to him that ordereth his way aright will I shew the salvation of God.

FIFTY-NINTH LESSON.

HAB. 3.   O LORD, I have heard the report of thee, and am afraid:
O Lord, revive thy work in the midst of the years,

In the midst of the years make it known;
In wrath remember mercy.

God came from Teman,
And the Holy One from mount Paran.

His glory covered the heavens,
And the earth was full of his praise.

And *his* brightness was as the light; he had rays *coming forth* from his hand:
And there was the hiding of his power.

Before him went the pestilence,
And fiery bolts went forth at his feet.

He stood, and measured the earth;
  He beheld, and drove asunder the nations:
And the eternal mountains were scattered, the everlasting hills did bow;
  His goings were as of old.
I saw the tents of Cushan in affliction:
  The curtains of the land of Midian did tremble.
Was the Lord displeased against the rivers?
  Was thine anger against the rivers, or thy wrath against the sea,
That thou didst ride upon thine horses,
  Upon thy chariots of salvation?
Thy bow was made quite bare;
  The oaths to the tribes were a sure word.
Thou didst cleave the earth with rivers.
  The mountains saw thee, and were afraid;
The tempest of waters passed by:
  The deep uttered his voice, and lifted up his hands on high.
The sun and moon stood still in their habitation;
  At the light of thine arrows as they went, at the shining of thy glittering spear.
Thou didst march through the land in indignation,
  Thou didst thresh the nations in anger.
Thou wentest forth for the salvation of thy people,
  For the salvation of thine anointed;
Thou woundedst the head out of the house of the wicked,
  Laying bare the foundation even unto the neck.
Thou didst pierce with his own staves the head of his warriors:
  They came as a whirlwind to scatter me: their rejoicing was as to devour the poor secretly.
Thou didst tread the sea with thine horses,
  The heap of mighty waters.
I heard, and my belly trembled, my lips quivered at the voice;
  Rottenness entered into my bones, and I trembled in my place:
That I should rest in the day of trouble,
  When it cometh up against the people which invadeth him in troops.
For though the fig tree shall not blossom,
  Neither shall fruit be in the vines;

The labor of the olive shall fail,
  And the fields shall yield no meat:
The flock shall be cut off from the fold,
  And there shall be no herd in the stalls:
Yet I will rejoice in the Lord,
  I will joy in the God of my salvation.
Jehovah, the Lord, is my strength, and he maketh my feet like hinds' *feet*,
  And will make me to walk upon mine high places.

SIXTIETH LESSON.

Ps. 9. I WILL give thanks unto the Lord with my whole heart;
  I will shew forth all thy marvellous works.
I will be glad and exult in thee:
  I will sing praise to thy name, O thou Most High.
When mine enemies turn back,
  They stumble and perish at thy presence.
For thou hast maintained my right and my cause;
  Thou satest in the throne judging righteously.
Thou hast rebuked the nations, thou hast destroyed the wicked,
  Thou hast blotted out their name for ever and ever.
The enemy are come to an end, they are desolate for ever;
  And the cities which thou hast overthrown, their very memorial is perished.
But the Lord sitteth *as king* for ever:
  He hath prepared his throne for judgment.
And he shall judge the world in righteousness,
  He shall minister judgment to the peoples in uprightness.
The Lord also will be a high tower for the oppressed,
  A high tower in times of trouble.
And they that know thy name will put their trust in thee;
  For thou, Lord, hast not forsaken them that seek thee.
Sing praises to the Lord, which dwelleth in Zion:
  Declare among the people his doings.
For he that maketh inquisition for blood remembereth them:
  He forgetteth not the cry of the poor.

Have mercy upon me, O Lord; behold my affliction *which I suffer* of them that hate me,
   Thou that liftest me up from the gates of death;
That I may shew forth all thy praise:
   In the gates of the daughter of Zion, I will rejoice in thy salvation.
The nations are sunk down in the pit that they made:
   In the net which they hid is their own foot taken.
The Lord hath made himself known, he hath executed judgment:
   The wicked is snared in the work of his own hands.
The wicked shall be turned back unto Sheol,
   Even all the nations that forget God.
For the needy shall not alway be forgotten,
   Nor the expectation of the poor perish for ever.
Arise, O Lord; let not man prevail:
   Let the nations be judged in thy sight.
Put them in fear, O Lord:
   Let the nations know themselves to be but men.

SIXTY-FIRST LESSON.

Ps. 119.   Blessed are they that are perfect in the way,
   Who walk in the law of the Lord.
Blessed are they that keep his testimonies,
   That seek him with the whole heart.
Oh that my ways were established to observe thy statutes!
   Then shall I not be ashamed, when I have respect unto all thy commandments.
Wherewithal shall a young man cleanse his way?
   By taking heed thereto according to thy word.
With my whole heart have I sought thee:
   O let me not wander from thy commandments.
Thy word have I laid up in mine heart, that I might not sin against thee.
   I have rejoiced in the way of thy testimonies, as much as in all riches.
I will meditate in thy precepts,
   And have respect unto thy ways.
Open thou mine eyes, that I may behold wondrous things out of thy law.
   Thy testimonies also are my delight and my counsellors.

THE WAY OF WISDOM.

Teach me, O Lord, the way of thy statutes;
    And I shall keep it unto the end.

Give me understanding, and I shall keep thy law;
    Yea, I shall observe it with my whole heart.

Make me to go in the path of thy commandments;
    For therein do I delight.

Incline my heart unto thy testimonies, and not to covetousness.
    Thy statutes have been my songs in the house of my pilgrimage.

I have remembered thy name, O Lord, in the night,
    And have observed thy law.

I am a companion of all them that fear thee,
    And of them that observe thy precepts.

Before I was afflicted I went astray;
    But now I observe thy word.

It is good for me that I have been afflicted; that I might learn thy statutes.
    The law of thy mouth is better unto me than thousands of gold and silver.

I know, O Lord, that thy judgments are righteous,
    And that in faithfulness thou hast afflicted me.

Let, I pray thee, thy loving-kindness be for my comfort,
    According to thy word unto thy servant.

For ever, O Lord, thy word is settled in heaven.
    Thy faithfulness is unto all generations:

Thou hast established the earth, and it abideth. They abide this day according to thine ordinances;
    For all things are thy servants.

Unless thy law had been my delight,
    I should then have perished in mine affliction.

I will never forget thy precepts;
    For with them thou hast quickened me.

I am thine, save me;
    For I have sought thy precepts.

The wicked have waited for me to destroy me;
    But I will consider thy testimonies.

I have seen an end of all perfection;
    But thy commandment is exceeding broad.

SIXTY-SECOND LESSON.

Ps. 119. Oh how love I thy law!
It is my meditation all the day.
Thy commandments make me wiser than mine enemies;
For they are ever with me.
How sweet are thy words unto my taste!
Yea, sweeter than honey to my mouth!
Through thy precepts I get understanding:
Therefore I hate every false way.
Thy word is a lamp unto my feet, and light unto my path.
I have sworn, and have confirmed it, that I will observe thy righteous judgments.
Thy testimonies have I taken as an heritage for ever;
For they are the rejoicing of my heart.
I have inclined mine heart to perform thy statutes, for ever, even unto the end.
Thou art my hiding place and my shield: I hope in thy word.
Depart from me, ye evil-doers;
That I may keep the commandments of my God.
It is time for the Lord to work; *for* they have made void thy law.
Therefore I love thy commandments above gold, yea, above fine gold.
Therefore I esteem all *thy* precepts concerning all *things* to be right;
And I hate every false way.
Thy testimonies are wonderful:
Therefore doth my soul keep them.
The opening of thy words giveth light;
It giveth understanding unto the simple.
Order my footsteps in thy word;
And let not any iniquity have dominion over me.
Make thy face to shine upon thy servant;
And teach me thy statutes.
Righteous art thou, O Lord, and upright are thy judgments.
Thou hast commanded thy testimonies in righteousness and very faithfulness.
Thy righteousness is an everlasting righteousness,
And thy law is truth.
Consider how I love thy precepts:
Quicken me, O Lord, according to thy loving-kindness.

The sum of thy word is truth;
: And every one of thy righteous judgments endureth for ever.

Great peace have they which love thy law;
: And they have none occasion of stumbling.

I have hoped for thy salvation, O Lord, and have done thy commandments.
: My soul hath observed thy testimonies; and I love them exceedingly.

I have observed thy precepts and thy testimonies;
: For all my ways are before thee.

Let my cry come near before thee, O Lord:
: Give me understanding according to thy word.

Let my supplication come before thee:
: Deliver me according to thy word.

SIXTY-THIRD LESSON.

PROV. 3. My son, forget not my law; but let thine heart keep my commandments:
: For length of days, and years of life, and peace, shall they add to thee.

Let not mercy and truth forsake thee:
: Bind them about thy neck;

Write them upon the table of thine heart:
: So shalt thou find favor and good understanding in the sight of God and man.

Trust in the Lord with all thine heart,
: And lean not upon thine own understanding:

In all thy ways acknowledge him,
: And he shall direct thy paths.

Be not wise in thine own eyes; fear the Lord, and depart from evil:
: It shall be health to thy navel, and marrow to thy bones.

Honor the Lord with thy substance,
: And with the first fruits of all thine increase:

So shall thy barns be filled with plenty,
: And thy fats shall overflow with new wine.

My son, despise not the chastening of the Lord;
: Neither be weary of his reproof:

For whom the Lord loveth he reproveth;
: Even as a father the son in whom he delighteth.

Happy is the man that findeth wisdom,
  And the man that getteth understanding.
For the merchandise of it is better than the merchandise of silver,
  And the gain thereof than fine gold.
She is more precious than rubies:
  And none of the things thou canst desire are to be compared unto her.
Length of days is in her right hand;
  In her left hand are riches and honor.
Her ways are ways of pleasantness,
  And all her paths are peace.
She is a tree of life to them that lay hold upon her:
  And happy is every one that retaineth her.
The Lord by wisdom founded the earth;
  By understanding he established the heavens.
By his knowledge the depths were broken up,
  And the skies drop down the dew.
My son, let not them depart from thine eyes; keep sound wisdom and discretion;
  So shall they be life unto thy soul, and grace to thy neck.
Then shalt thou walk in thy way securely,
  And thy foot shall not stumble.
When thou liest down, thou shalt not be afraid:
  Yea, thou shalt lie down, and thy sleep shall be sweet.
Be not afraid of sudden fear,
  Neither of the desolation of the wicked, when it cometh:
For the Lord shall be thy confidence,
  And shall keep thy foot from being taken.

SIXTY-FOURTH LESSON.

PROV. 4. HEAR, *my* sons, the instruction of a father,
  And attend to know understanding:
For I give you good doctrine;
  Forsake ye not my law.
For I was a son unto my father,
  Tender and only beloved in the sight of my mother.

THE WAY OF WISDOM.

And he taught me, and said unto me, let thine heart retain my words;
Keep my commandments, and live:
Get wisdom, get understanding;
Forget it not, neither decline from the words of my mouth:
Forsake her not, and she shall preserve thee;
Love her, and she shall keep thee.
Wisdom *is* the principal thing; *therefore* get wisdom:
Yea, with all thy getting get understanding.
Exalt her, and she shall promote thee:
She shall bring thee to honor, when thou dost embrace her.
She shall give to thine head a chaplet of grace:
A crown of beauty shall she deliver to thee.
Hear, O my son, and receive my sayings;
And the years of thy life shall be many.
I have taught thee in the way of wisdom;
I have led thee in paths of uprightness.
When thou goest, thy steps shall not be straitened;
And if thou runnest, thou shalt not stumble.
Take fast hold of instruction; let her not go:
Keep her; for she is thy life.
Enter not into the path of the wicked,
And walk not in the way of evil men.
Avoid it, pass not by it;
Turn from it, and pass on.
For they sleep not, except they have done mischief;
And their sleep is taken away, unless they cause some to fall.
For they eat the bread of wickedness,
And drink the wine of violence.
But the path of the righteous is as the dawning light,
That shineth more and more unto the perfect day.
The way of the wicked is as darkness:
They know not at what they stumble.
My son, attend to my words;
Incline thine ear unto my sayings.
Let them not depart from thine eyes;
Keep them in the midst of thine heart.

THE WAY OF WISDOM.

For they are life unto those that find them,
  And health to all their flesh.
Keep thy heart with all diligence;
  For out of it are the issues of life.
Put away from thee a froward mouth,
  And perverse lips put far from thee.
Let thine eyes look right on,
  And let thine eyelids look straight before thee.
Make level the path of thy feet,
  And let all thy ways be established.
Turn not to the right hand nor to the left:
  Remove thy foot from evil.

SIXTY-FIFTH LESSON.

PROV. 8. DOTH not wisdom cry, and understanding put forth her voice?
  In the top of high places by the way, where the paths meet, she standeth;
Beside the gates, at the entry of the city,
  At the coming in at the doors, she crieth aloud:
Unto you, O men, I call;
  And my voice is to the sons of men.
O ye simple, understand subtilty;
  And, ye fools, be ye of an understanding heart.
Hear, for I will speak excellent things;
  And the opening of my lips shall be right things.
For my mouth shall utter truth;
  And wickedness is an abomination to my lips.
All the words of my mouth are in righteousness;
  There is nothing crooked or perverse in them.
They are all plain to him that understandeth,
  And right to them that find knowledge.
Receive my instruction, and not silver;
  And knowledge rather than choice gold.
For wisdom is better than rubies;
  And all the things that may be desired are not to be compared unto her.

THE WAY OF WISDOM.

Counsel is mine, and sound knowledge:
　I am understanding; I have might.

By me kings reign, and princes decree justice.
　By me princes rule, and nobles, even all the judges of the earth.

I love them that love me;
　And those that seek me diligently shall find me.

Riches and honor are with me;
　Yea, durable riches and righteousness.

My fruit is better than gold, yea, than fine gold;
　And my revenue than choice silver.

I walk in the way of righteousness,
　In the midst of the paths of judgment:

That I may cause those that love me to inherit substance,
　And that I may fill their treasuries.

The Lord possessed me in the beginning of his way, before his works of old.
　I was set up from everlasting, from the beginning, or ever the earth was.

When there were no depths, I was brought forth;
　When there were no fountains abounding with water.

Before the mountains were settled,
　Before the hills was I brought forth:

While as yet he had not made the earth, nor the fields,
　Nor the beginning of the dust of the world.

When he established the heavens, I was there:
　When he set a circle upon the face of the deep:

When he made firm the skies above:
　When the fountains of the deep became strong:

When he gave to the sea its bound,
　That the waters should not transgress his commandment:

When he marked out the foundations of the earth:
　Then I was by him, as a master workman:

And I was daily *his* delight,
　Rejoicing always before him;

Rejoicing in his habitable earth;
　And my delight was with the sons of men.

Now therefore, *my* sons, hearken unto me: for blessed are they that keep my ways.
Hear instruction, and be wise, and refuse it not.
Blessed is the man that heareth me,
Watching daily at my gates, waiting at the posts of my doors.
For whoso findeth me findeth life,
And shall obtain favor of the Lord.
But he that sinneth against me wrongeth his own soul:
All they that hate me love death.

SIXTY-SIXTH LESSON.

PROV. 14. The wisdom of the prudent is to understand his way:
But the folly of fools is deceit.
The foolish make a mock at guilt
But among the upright there is good will.
The heart knoweth its own bitterness;
And a stranger doth not intermeddle with its joy.
The house of the wicked shall be overthrown:
But the tent of the upright shall flourish.
There is a way which seemeth right unto a man,
But the end thereof are the ways of death.
Even in laughter the heart is sorrowful;
And the end of mirth is heaviness.
The backslider in heart shall be filled with his own ways:
And a good man shall be satisfied from himself.
The simple believeth every word:
But the prudent man looketh well to his going.
A wise man feareth, and departeth from evil:
But the fool beareth himself insolently, and is confident.
He that is soon angry will deal foolishly:
And a man of wicked devices is hated.
The simple inherit folly:
But the prudent are crowned with knowledge.
The evil bow before the good;
And the wicked at the gates of the righteous.

THE WAY OF WISDOM.

The poor is hated even of his own neighbor:
> But the rich hath many friends.

He that despiseth his neighbor sinneth:
> But he that hath pity on the poor, happy is he.

Do they not err that devise evil?
> But mercy and truth shall be to them that devise good.

In all labor there is profit:
> But the talk of the lips tendeth only to penury.

The crown of the wise is their riches:
> But the folly of fools is only folly.

A true witness delivereth souls:
> But he that uttereth lies causeth deceit.

In the fear of the Lord is strong confidence:
> And his children shall have a place of refuge

The fear of the Lord is a fountain of life,
> To depart from the snares of death.

In the multitude of people is the king's glory:
> But in the want of people is the destruction of the prince.

He that is slow to anger is of great understanding:
> But he that is hasty of spirit exalteth folly.

A sound heart is the life of the flesh:
> But envy is the rottenness of the bones.

He that oppresseth the poor reproacheth his Maker:
> But he that hath mercy on the needy honoreth him.

The wicked is thrust down in his evil-doing:
> But the righteous hath hope in his death.

Wisdom resteth in the heart of him that hath understanding:
> But that which is in the inward part of fools is made known.

Righteousness exalteth a nation:
> But sin is a reproach to any people.

The king's favor is toward a servant that dealeth wisely:
> But his wrath shall be against him that causeth shame.

THE MESSIAH AND HIS KINGDOM.
SIXTY-SEVENTH LESSON.

Ps. 2. Why do the nations rage, and the peoples meditate a vain thing?
The kings of the earth set themselves,
And the rulers take counsel together, against the Lord, and against his anointed, *saying,*
Let us break their bands asunder, and cast away their chords from us.
He that sitteth in the heavens shall laugh:
The Lord shall have them in derision.
Then shall he speak unto them in his wrath, and vex them in his sore displeasure;
Yet I have set my king upon my holy hill of Zion.
I will tell of the decree: the Lord said unto me, Thou art my son;
This day have I begotten thee.
Ask of me, and I will give *thee* the nations for thine inheritance,
And the uttermost parts of the earth for thy possession.
Thou shalt break them with a rod of iron;
Thou shalt dash them in pieces like a potter's vessel.
Now therefore be wise, O ye kings: be instructed, ye judges of the earth.
Serve the Lord with fear, and rejoice with trembling.
Kiss the son, lest he be angry, and ye perish in the way, for his wrath will soon be kindled.
Blessed are all they that put their trust in him.

Ps. 110. The Lord saith unto my lord, Sit thou at my right hand,
Until I make thine enemies thy footstool.
The Lord shall stretch forth the rod of thy strength out of Zion:
Rule thou in the midst of thine enemies.
Thy people offer themselves willingly in the day of thy power:
In holy attire; out of the womb of the morning, thou hast the dew of thy youth.
The Lord hath sworn, and will not repent,
Thou art a priest for ever after the order of Melchizedek.
The Lord at thy right hand shall strike through kings in the day of his wrath.
He shall judge among the nations,
He shall fill *the places* with dead bodies;
He shall strike through the head in many countries.
He shall drink of the brook in the way:
Therefore shall he lift up the head.

Ps. 76. In Judah is God known:
His name is great in Israel.
In Salem also is his tabernacle,
And his dwelling place in Zion.
There he brake the arrows of the bow;
The shield, and the sword, and the battle.
Glorious art thou *and* excellent, from the mountains of prey. The stouthearted are spoiled,
They have slept their sleep; and none of the men of might have found their hands.
At thy rebuke, O God of Jacob,
Both chariot and horse are cast into a dead sleep.
Thou, even thou, art to be feared;
And who may stand in thy sight when once thou art angry?
Thou didst cause sentence to be heard from heaven; the earth feared, and was still,
When God arose to judgment, to save all the meek of the earth.
Surely the wrath of man shall praise thee:
The residue of wrath shalt thou gird upon thee.
Vow, and pay unto the Lord your God:
Let all that be round about him bring presents unto him that ought to be feared.
He shall cut off the spirit of princes:
He is terrible to the kings of the earth.

SIXTY-EIGHTH LESSON.

Ps. 16. Preserve me, O God: for in thee do I put my trust.
O my soul, thou hast said unto the Lord, Thou art my Lord; I have no good beyond thee.
As for the saints that are in the earth,
They are the excellent in whom is all my delight.
Their sorrows shall be multiplied that give gifts for another *god:*
Their drink offerings of blood will I not offer, nor take their names upon my lips.
The Lord is the portion of mine inheritance and of my cup:
Thou maintainest my lot.
The lines are fallen unto me in pleasant places;
Yea, I have a goodly heritage.

I will bless the Lord, who hath given me counsel:
  Yea, my reins instruct me in the night seasons.
I have set the Lord always before me:
  Because he is at my right hand, I shall not be moved.
Therefore my heart is glad, and my glory rejoiceth:
  My flesh also shall dwell in safety.
For thou wilt not leave my soul to Sheol;
  Neither wilt thou suffer thine holy one to see corruption.
Thou wilt shew me the path of life: in thy presence is fulness of joy;
  In thy right hand there are pleasures for evermore.

Ps. 21. The king shall joy in thy strength, O Lord;
  And in thy salvation how greatly shall he rejoice!
Thou hast given him his heart's desire,
  And hast not withholden the request of his lips.
For thou meetest him with the blessings of goodness:
  Thou settest a crown of fine gold on his head.
He asked life of thee, thou gavest it him;
  Even length of days for ever and ever.
His glory is great in thy salvation:
  Honor and majesty dost thou lay upon him.
For thou makest him most blessed for ever:
  Thou makest him glad with joy in thy presence.
For the king trusteth in the Lord,
  And through the loving-kindness of the Most High he shall not be moved.
Thine hand shall find out all thine enemies: thy right hand shall find out those that hate thee.
  Thou shalt make them as a fiery furnace in the time of thine anger.
The Lord shall swallow them up in his wrath,
  And the fire shall devour them.
Their fruit shalt thou destroy from the earth,
  And their seed from among the children of men.
For they intended evil against thee:
  They imagined a device which they are not able to perform.
For thou shalt make them turn their back,
  Thou shalt make ready with thy bowstrings against the face of them.
Be thou exalted, O Lord, in thy strength:
  So will we sing and praise thy power.

SIXTY-NINTH LESSON.

Ps. 22. My God, my God, why hast thou forsaken me?
Why art thou so far from helping me, and from the words of my roaring?
O my God, I cry in the day-time, but thou answerest not;
And in the night season, and am not silent.
But thou art holy,
O thou that inhabitest the praises of Israel.
Our fathers trusted in thee:
They trusted, and thou didst deliver them.
They cried unto thee, and were delivered:
They trusted in thee, and were not ashamed.
But I am a worm, and no man;
A reproach of men, and despised of the people.
All they that see me laugh me to scorn:
They shoot out the lip, they shake the head, saying, Commit thyself unto the Lord;
Let him deliver him:
Let him rescue him, seeing he delighteth in him.
But thou art he that took me out of the womb:
Thou didst make me trust when I was upon my mother's breasts.
I was cast upon thee from the womb:
Thou art my God since my mother bare me.
Be not far from me; for trouble is near;
For there is none to help.
Many bulls have compassed me:
Strong bulls of Bashan have beset me round.
They gape upon me with their mouth,
As a ravening and a roaring lion.
I am poured out like water,
And all my bones are out of joint:
My heart is like wax;
It is melted in the midst of my bowels.
My strength is dried up like a potsherd; and my tongue cleaveth to my jaws;
And thou hast brought me into the dust of death.
For dogs have compassed me: the assembly of evil-doers have inclosed me;
They pierced my hands and my feet.

I may tell all my bones;
They look and stare upon me:
They part my garments among them,
And upon my vesture do they cast lots.
But be not thou far off, O Lord:
O thou my succor, haste thee to help me.
Deliver my soul from the sword;
My darling from the power of the dog.
Save me from the lion's mouth;
Yea, from the horns of the wild-oxen thou hast answered me.
I will declare thy name unto my brethren:
In the midst of the congregation will I praise thee.
Ye that fear the Lord, praise him; all ye the seed of Jacob, glorify him;
And stand in awe of him, all ye the seed of Israel.
For he hath not despised nor abhorred the affliction of the afflicted·
Neither hath he hid his face from him; but when he cried unto him, he heard.
Of thee cometh my praise in the great congregation:
I will pay my vows before them that fear him
The meek shall eat and be satisfied: they shall praise the Lord that seek after him:
Let your heart live for ever.
All the ends of the earth shall remember and turn unto the Lord:
And all the kindreds of the nations shall worship before thee.
For the kingdom is the Lord's:
And he is the ruler over the nations.
All the fat ones of the earth shall eat and worship:
All they that go down to the dust shall bow before him, even he that cannot keep his soul alive.
A seed shall serve him; it shall be told of the Lord unto the *next* generation.
They shall come and shall declare his righteousness unto a people that shall be born, that he hath done it.

SEVENTIETH LESSON.

Ps. 45. My heart overfloweth with a goodly matter: I speak the things which I have made touching the king:
My tongue is the pen of a ready writer.
Thou art fairer than the children of men; grace is poured into thy lips:
Therefore God hath blessed thee for ever.
Gird thy sword upon thy thigh, O mighty one, thy glory and thy majesty.
And in thy majesty ride on prosperously,
Because of truth and meekness *and* righteousness:
And thy right hand shall teach thee terrible things.
Thine arrows are sharp; the peoples fall under thee;
They are in the heart of the king's enemies.
Thy throne, O God, is for ever and ever:
A sceptre of equity is the sceptre of thy kingdom.
Thou hast loved righteousness, and hated wickedness:
Therefore God, thy God, hath anointed thee with the oil of gladness above thy fellows.
All thy garments *smell of* myrrh, and aloes, *and* cassia;
Out of ivory palaces stringed instruments have made thee glad.
Kings' daughters are among thy honorable women:
At thy right hand doth stand the queen in gold of Ophir.
Hearken, O daughter, and consider, and incline thine ear;
Forget also thine own people, and thy father's house;
So shall the king desire thy beauty:
For he is thy Lord; and worship thou him.
And the daughter of Tyre *shall be there* with a gift;
Even the rich among the people shall intreat thy favor.
The king's daughter within *the palace* is all glorious:
Her clothing is inwrought with gold.
She shall be led unto the king in broidered work:
The virgins her companions that follow her shall be brought unto thee.
With gladness and rejoicing shall they be led:
They shall enter into the king's palace.
Instead of thy fathers shall be thy children,
Whom thou shalt make princes in all the earth.

I will make thy name to be remembered in all generations:
Therefore shall the peoples give thee thanks for ever and ever.

Ps. 98. O SING unto the Lord a new song; for he hath done marvellous things:
His right hand, and his holy arm, hath wrought salvation for him.

The Lord hath made known his salvation:
His righteousness hath he openly shewed in the sight of the nations.

He hath remembered his mercy and his faithfulness toward the house of Israel:
All the ends of the earth have seen the salvation of our God.

Make a joyful noise unto the Lord, all the earth:
Break forth and sing for joy, yea, sing praises.

Sing praises unto the Lord with the harp; with the harp and the voice of melody.
With trumpets and sound of cornet make a joyful noise before the King, the Lord.

Let the sea roar, and the fulness thereof;
The world, and they that dwell therein;

Let the floods clap their hands;
Let the hills sing for joy together;

Before the Lord, for he cometh to judge the earth,
He shall judge the world with righteousness, and the peoples with equity.

SEVENTY-FIRST LESSON.

Ps. 68. LET God arise, let his enemies be scattered;
Let them also that hate him flee before him.

As smoke is driven away, so drive them away:
As wax melteth before the fire, so let the wicked perish at the presence of God.

But let the righteous be glad; let them exult before God.
Yea, let them rejoice with gladness.

Sing unto God, sing praises to his name: cast up a highway for him that rideth through the deserts;
His name is Jah; and exult ye before him.

A father of the fatherless, and a judge of the widows, is God in his holy habitation.
God setteth the solitary in families:

He bringeth out the prisoners into prosperity:
  But the rebellious dwell in a parched land.
O God, when thou wentest forth before thy people,
  When thou didst march through the wilderness;
The earth trembled, the heavens also dropped at the presence of God:
  Even that Sinai trembled at the presence of God, the God of Israel.
Thou, O God, didst send a plentiful rain,
  Thou didst confirm thine inheritance, when it was weary.
Thy congregation dwelt therein:
  Thou, O God, didst prepare of thy goodness for the poor.
The Lord giveth the word:
  The women that publish the tidings are a great host.
Kings of armies flee, they flee:
  And she that tarrieth at home divideth the spoil.
When ye lie among the sheepfolds,
  It is as the wings of a dove covered with silver,
And her pinions with yellow gold.
  When the Almighty scattereth kings therein, it was as when it snoweth in Zalmon.
A mountain of God is the mountain of Bashan;
  An high mountain is the mountain of Bashan.
Why look ye askance, ye high mountains, at the mountain which God hath desired for his abode?
  Yea, the Lord will dwell in it for ever.
The chariots of God are twenty thousand, even thousands upon thousands:
  The Lord is among them, as in Sinai, in the sanctuary.
Thou hast ascended on high, thou hast led away captives;
  Thou hast received gifts among men, yea, among the rebellious also, that the Lord God might dwell with them.
Blessed be the Lord, who daily beareth our burden,
  Even the God who is our salvation.
God is unto us a God of deliverances;
  And unto JEHOVAH the Lord belongeth escape from death.
But God shall smite through the head of his enemies,
  The hairy scalp of such an one as goeth on still in his guiltiness.
The Lord said, I will bring again from Bashan,
  I will bring them again from the depths of the sea:

That thou mayest crush them dipping thy foot in blood.
  That the tongue of thy dogs may have its portion from thine enemies.
They have seen thy goings, O God,
  Even the goings of my God, my King, into the sanctuary.
The singers went before, the minstrels followed after,
  In the midst of the damsels playing with timbrels.
Bless ye God in the congregations,
  Even the Lord, ye that are of the fountain of Israel.
There is little Benjamin their ruler, the princes of Judah *and* their council,
  The princes of Zebulun, the princes of Naphtali.
Thy God hath commanded thy strength:
  Strengthen, O God, that which thou hast wrought for us.
Because of thy temple at Jerusalem
  Kings shall bring presents unto thee.
Rebuke the wild beast of the reeds,
  The multitude of the bulls, with the calves of the peoples,
Trampling under foot the pieces of silver;
  He hath scattered the peoples that delight in war.
Princes shall come out of Egypt;
  Ethiopia shall haste to stretch out her hands unto God.
Sing unto God, ye kingdoms of the earth;
  O sing praises unto the Lord.
To him that rideth upon the heaven of heavens, which are of old;
  Lo, he uttereth his voice, and that a mighty voice.
Ascribe ye strength unto God:
  His excellency is over Israel, and his strength is in the skies.
O God, *thou art* terrible out of thy holy places: the God of Israel, he giveth strength and power unto *his* people.
  Blessed be God.

SEVENTY-SECOND LESSON.

Ps. 72. GIVE the king thy judgments, O God, and thy righteousness unto the king's son.
He shall judge thy people with righteousness, and thy poor with judgment.
The mountains shall bring peace to the people,
And the hills, in righteousness.
He shall judge the poor of the people, he shall save the children of the needy,
And shall break in pieces the oppressor.
They shall fear thee while the sun endureth,
And so long as the moon, throughout all generations.
He shall come down like rain upon the mown grass:
As showers that water the earth.
· In his days shall the righteous flourish;
And abundance of peace, till the moon be no more.
He shall have dominion also from sea to sea,
And from the River unto the ends of the earth.
They that dwell in the wilderness shall bow before him;
And his enemies shall lick the dust.
The kings of Tarshish and of the isles shall bring presents:
The kings of Sheba and Seba shall offer gifts.
Yea, all kings shall fall down before him:
All nations shall serve him.
For he shall deliver the needy when he crieth;
And the poor, that hath no helper.
He shall have pity on the poor and needy,
And the souls of the needy he shall save.
He shall redeem their soul from oppression and violence;
And precious shall their blood be in his sight:
And they shall live; and to him shall be given of the gold of Sheba:
And men shall pray for him continually; they shall bless him all the day long.
There shall be abundance of corn in the earth upon the top of the mountains; the fruit thereof shall shake like Lebanon:
And they of the city shall flourish like grass of the earth.
His name shall endure for ever;
His name shall be continued as long as the sun:

And men shall be blessed in him ;
  All nations shall call him happy.
Blessed be the Lord God, the God of Israel, who only doeth wondrous things :
  And blessed be his glorious name for ever;
And let the whole earth be filled with his glory.
  Amen, and Amen.

Ps. 67. GOD be merciful unto us, and bless us,
  And cause his face to shine upon us;
That thy way may be known upon earth,
  Thy salvation among all nations.
Let the peoples praise thee, O God ;
  Let all the peoples praise thee.
O let the nations be glad and sing for joy :
  For thou shalt judge the peoples with equity, and govern the nations upon earth.
Let the peoples praise thee, O God ;
  Let all the peoples praise thee.
The earth hath yielded her increase :
  God, even our own God, shall bless us.
God shall bless us ;
  And all the ends of the earth shall fear him.

SEVENTY-THIRD LESSON.

ISA. 11: 1-9. AND there shall come forth a shoot out of the stock of Jesse,
  And a branch out of his roots shall bear fruit:
And the Spirit of the Lord shall rest upon him,
  The spirit of wisdom and understanding,
The spirit of counsel and might, the spirit of knowledge and of the fear of the Lord ;
  And his delight shall be in the fear of the Lord:
And he shall not judge after the sight of his eyes,
  Neither decide after the hearing of his ears:
But with righteousness shall he judge the poor,
  And decide with equity for the meek of the earth.

And he shall smite the earth with the rod of his mouth,
And with the breath of his lips shall he slay the wicked.

And righteousness shall be the girdle of his loins,
And faithfulness the girdle of his reins.

And the wolf shall dwell with the lamb,
And the leopard shall lie down with the kid;

And the calf, and the young lion, and the fatling together;
And a little child shall lead them.

And the cow and the bear shall feed; their young ones shall lie down together:
And the lion shall eat straw like the ox.

And the sucking child shall play on the hole of the asp,
And the weaned child shall put his hand on the basilisk's den.

They shall not hurt nor destroy in all my holy mountain:
For the earth shall be full of the knowledge of the Lord, as the waters cover the sea.

ISA. 35. THE wilderness and the solitary place shall be glad;
And the desert shall rejoice, and blossom as the rose.

It shall blossom abundantly,
And rejoice even with joy and singing;

The glory of Lebanon shall be given unto it, the excellency of Carmel and Sharon:
They shall see the glory of the Lord, the excellency of our God.

Strengthen ye the weak hands, and confirm the feeble knees.
Say to them that are of a fearful heart, Be strong, fear not:

Behold, your God will come *with* vengeance, *with* the recompense of God;
He will come and save you.

Then the eyes of the blind shall be opened,
And the ears of the deaf shall be unstopped.

Then shall the lame man leap as an hart, and the tongue of the dumb shall sing:
For in the wilderness shall waters break out, and streams in the desert.

And the glowing sand shall become a pool, and the thirsty ground springs of water:
In the habitation of jackals, where they lay, shall be grass with reeds and rushes.

And an highway shall be there, and a way,
  And it shall be called The way of holiness;
The unclean shall not pass over it; but it shall be for those:
  The wayfaring men, yea fools, shall not err therein.
No lion shall be there, nor shall any ravenous beast go up thereon, they shall not be found there;
  But the redeemed shall walk there;
And the ransomed of the Lord shall return, and come with singing unto Zion; and everlasting joy shall be upon their heads:
  They shall obtain gladness and joy, and sorrow and sighing shall flee away.

SEVENTY-FOURTH LESSON.

ISA. 9.   THE people that walked in darkness have seen a great light:
  They that dwelt in the land of the shadow of death, upon them hath the light shined.
Thou hast multiplied the nation, thou hast increased their joy:
  They joy before thee according to the joy in harvest, as men rejoice when they divide the spoil.
For unto us a child is born, unto us a son is given: and the government shall be upon his shoulder:
  And his name shall be called Wonderful, Counsellor, Mighty God, Everlasting Father, Prince of Peace.
Of the increase of his government and of peace there shall be no end,
  Upon the throne of David, and upon his kingdom,
To establish it, and to uphold it with judgment and with righteousness from henceforth even for ever.
  The zeal of the Lord of hosts shall perform this.

ISA. 42.   BEHOLD my servant, whom I uphold;
  My chosen, in whom my soul delighteth:
I have put my spirit upon him; he shall bring forth judgment to the Gentiles:
  He shall not cry, nor lift up, nor cause his voice to be heard in the street.
A bruised reed shall he not break, and the smoking flax shall he not quench:
  He shall bring forth judgment in truth.
He shall not fail nor be discouraged, till he have set judgment in the earth;
  And the isles shall wait for his law.

Thus saith God the Lord, he that created the heavens, and stretched them forth;
He that spread abroad the earth and that which cometh out of it;
He that giveth bread unto the people upon it,
And spirit to them that walk therein:
I the Lord have called thee in righteousness, and will hold thine hand, and will keep thee,
And give thee for a covenant of the people, for a light of the Gentiles;
To open the blind eyes, to bring out the prisoners from the dungeon,
And them that sit in darkness out of the prison house.
I am the Lord; that is my name:
And my glory will I not give to another, neither my praise unto graven images.
Behold, the former things are come to pass, and new things do I declare:
Before they spring forth I tell you of them.
Sing unto the Lord a new song, and his praise from the end of the earth;
Ye that go down to the sea, and all that is therein, the isles, and the inhabitants thereof.
Let the wilderness and the cities thereof lift up *their voice*, the villages that Kedar doth inhabit;
Let the inhabitants of Sela sing, let them shout from the top of the mountains.
Let them give glory unto the Lord,
And declare his praise in the islands.

ISA. 12. AND in that day thou shalt say, I will give thanks unto thee, O Lord;
For though thou wast angry with me, thine anger is turned away, and thou comfortest me.
Behold, God is my salvation;
I will trust, and will not be afraid:
For the Lord Jehovah is my strength and song;
And he is become my salvation.
Therefore with joy shall ye draw water out of the wells of salvation.
And in that day shall ye say, Give thanks unto the Lord,
Call upon his name, declare his doings among the peoples,
Make mention that his name is exalted.
Sing unto the Lord; for he hath done excellent things:
Let this be known in all the earth.
Cry aloud and shout, thou inhabitant of Zion:
For great is the Holy One of Israel in the midst of thee.

THE MESSIAH AND HIS KINGDOM.

SEVENTY-FIFTH LESSON

ISA. 40. COMFORT ye, comfort ye my people, saith your God.
Speak ye comfortably to Jerusalem, and cry unto her
That her warfare is accomplished, that her iniquity is pardoned;
That she hath received of the Lord's hand double for all her sins.
The voice of one that crieth, Prepare ye in the wilderness the way of the Lord,
Make straight in the desert a high way for our God.
Every valley shall be exalted, and every mountain and hill shall be made low:
And the crooked shall be made straight, and the rough places plain:
And the glory of the Lord shall be revealed, and all flesh shall see it together:
For the mouth of the Lord hath spoken it.
The voice of one saying, Cry.
And one said, What shall I cry?
All flesh is grass, and all the goodliness thereof is as the flower of the field:
The grass withereth, the flower fadeth:
Because the breath of the Lord bloweth upon it:
Surely the people is grass.
The grass withereth, the flower fadeth:
But the word of our God shall stand for ever.
O thou that tellest good tidings to Zion, get thee up into the high mountain;
O thou that tellest good tidings to Jerusalem, lift up thy voice with strength;
Lift it up, be not afraid;
Say unto the cities of Judah, Behold, your God!
Behold, the Lord God will come as a mighty one, and his arm shall rule for him:
Behold, his reward is with him, and his recompence before him.
He shall feed his flock like a shepherd, he shall gather the lambs in his arm, and carry them in his bosom,
And shall gently lead those that give suck.

ISA. 60. ARISE, shine; for thy light is come,
And the glory of the Lord is risen upon thee.
For, behold, darkness shall cover the earth, and gross darkness the peoples:
But the Lord shall rise upon thee, and his glory shall be seen upon thee.
And nations shall come to thy light,
And kings to the brightness of thy rising.

Lift up thine eyes round about, and see: they all gather themselves together, they come to thee:
Thy sons shall come from far, and thy daughters shall be carried in the arms.

Then thou shalt see and be lightened, and thine heart shall tremble and be enlarged;
Because the abundance of the sea shall be turned unto thee, the wealth of the nations shall come unto thee.

Thy gates also shall be open continually; they shall not be shut day nor night;
That men may bring unto thee the wealth of the nations, and their kings led with them.

For that nation and kingdom that will not serve thee shall perish;
Yea, those nations shall be utterly wasted.

The glory of Lebanon shall come unto thee, the fir tree, the pine, and the box tree together;
To beautify the place of my sanctuary, and I will make the place of my feet glorious.

And the sons of them that afflicted thee shall come bending unto thee;
And all they that despised thee shall bow themselves down at the soles of thy feet;

And they shall call thee The city of the Lord,
The Zion of the Holy One of Israel.

Whereas thou hast been forsaken and hated, so that no man passed through thee,
I will make thee an eternal excellency, a joy of many generations.

Violence shall no more be heard in thy land, desolation nor destruction within thy borders;
But thou shalt call thy walls Salvation, and thy gates Praise.

The sun shall be no more thy light by day; neither for brightness shall the moon give light unto thee:
But the Lord shall be unto thee an everlasting light, and thy God thy glory.

Thy sun shall no more go down, neither shall thy moon withdraw itself:
For the Lord shall be thine everlasting light, and the days of thy mourning shall be ended.

Thy people also shall be all righteous, they shall inherit the land for ever·
The branch of my planting, the work of my hands, that I may be glorified.

The little one shall become a thousand, and the small one a strong nation:
I the Lord will hasten it in its time.

SEVENTY-SIXTH LESSON.

ISA. 53.   Who hath believed our message? and to whom hath the arm of the Lord been revealed?
For he grew up before him as a tender plant, and as a root out of a dry ground;
He hath no form or comelinesss;
And when we see him, there is no beauty that we should desire him.
He was despised, and rejected of men; a man of sorrows, and acquainted with grief:
And as one from whom men hide their face he was despised, and we esteemed him not.
Surely he hath borne our griefs, and carried our sorrows:
Yet we did esteem him stricken, smitten of God, and afflicted.
But he was wounded for our transgressions, he was bruised for our iniquities:
The chastisement of our peace was upon him; and with his stripes we are healed.
All we like sheep have gone astray; we have turned every one to his own way;
And the Lord hath laid on him the iniquity of us all.
He was oppressed, yet when he was afflicted he opened not his mouth; as a lamb that is led to the slaughter, and as a sheep that before her shearers is dumb;
So he opened not his mouth.
By oppression and judgment he was taken away; and as for his generation, who *among them* considered
That he was cut off out of the land of the living for the transgression of my people to whom the stroke was due?
And they made his grave with the wicked, and with a rich man in his death;
Although he had done no violence, neither was any deceit in his mouth.
Yet it pleased the Lord to bruise him;
He hath put him to grief:
When thou shalt make his soul an offering for sin, he shall see *his* seed, he shall prolong his days,
And the pleasure of the Lord shall prosper in his hand.
He shall see of the travail of his soul, *and* shall be satisfied: by the knowledge of himself shall my righteous servant justify many:
And he shall bear their iniquities.
Therefore will I divide him a portion with the great,
And he shall divide the spoil with the strong;

THE MESSIAH AND HIS KINGDOM.

Because he poured out his soul unto death, and was numbered with the transgressors :
Yet he bare the sin of many, and made intercession for the transgressors.

ZECH. 13. IN that day there shall be a fountain opened to the house of David
And to the inhabitants of Jerusalem, for sin and for uncleanness.

And one shall say unto him, What are these wounds between thine arms?
Then he shall answer, Those with which I was wounded in the house of my friends.

Awake, O sword, against my shepherd,
And against the man that is my fellow, saith the Lord of hosts:

Smite the shepherd, and the sheep shall be scattered ;
And I will turn mine hand upon the little ones.

And it shall come to pass, that in all the land, saith the Lord, two parts therein shall be cut off and die ;
But the third shall be left therein.

And I will bring the third part through the fire, and will refine them as silver is refined, and will try them as gold is tried:
They shall call on my name, and I will hear them:

I will say, It is my people ;
And they shall say, The Lord is my God.

SEVENTY-SEVENTH LESSON.

ISA. 61. THE spirit of the Lord God is upon me ;
Because the Lord hath anointed me to preach good tidings unto the meek;

He hath sent me to bind up the brokenhearted, to proclaim liberty to the captives,
And the opening of the prison to them that are bound ;

To proclaim the year of Jehovah's favor,
And the day of vengeance of our God:

To comfort all that mourn ; to appoint unto them that mourn in Zion,
To give unto them a garland for ashes, the oil of joy for mourning, the garment of praise for the spirit of heaviness ;

That they might be called trees of righteousness,
The planting of the Lord, that he might be glorified.

And they shall build the old wastes, they shall raise up the former desolations,
And they shall repair the waste cities, the desolations of many generations.

And strangers shall stand and feed your flocks,
And aliens shall be your plowmen and your vinedressers.

But ye shall be named the priests of the Lord:
Men shall call you the ministers of our God:

Ye shall eat the wealth of the nations,
And in their glory shall ye boast yourselves.

Instead of your shame ye shall have double;
And instead of dishonor they shall rejoice in their portion:

Therefore in their land they shall possess double:
Everlasting joy shall be unto them.

For I the Lord love judgment, I hate robbery with iniquity;
And I will give them their recompence in truth, and I will make an everlasting covenant with them.

And their seed shall be known among the nations,
And their offspring among the peoples:

All that see them shall acknowledge them,
That they are the seed which the Lord hath blessed.

I will greatly rejoice in the Lord, my soul shall be joyful in my God;
For he hath clothed me with the garments of salvation, he hath covered me with the robe of righteousness,

As a bridegroom decketh himself with a garland,
And as a bride adorneth herself with her jewels.

For as the earth bringeth forth her bud, and as the garden causeth the things that are sown in it to spring forth;
So the Lord God will cause righteousness and praise to spring forth before all the nations.

ISA. 51. Awake, awake, put on strength, O arm of the Lord;
Awake, as in the days of old, the generations of ancient times.

Art thou not it that cut Rahab in pieces,
That pierced the dragon

Art thou not it which dried up the sea, the waters of the great deep;
That made the depths of the sea a way for the redeemed to pass over?

And the ransomed of the Lord shall return, and come with singing unto Zion;
and everlasting joy shall be upon their heads:
They shall obtain gladness and joy, and sorrow and sighing shall flee away.

ISA. 52. Awake, awake, put on thy strength, O Zion; put on thy beautiful garments,
O Jerusalem, the holy city:
For henceforth there shall no more come into thee the uncircumcised and the unclean.
How beautiful upon the mountains are the feet of him that bringeth good tidings, that publisheth peace,
That bringeth good tidings of good, that publisheth salvation; that saith unto Zion, Thy God reigneth!
The voice of the watchmen! they lift up the voice, together do they sing;
For they shall see, eye to eye, when the Lord returneth to Zion.
Break forth into joy, sing together, ye waste places of Jerusalem:
For the Lord hath comforted his people, he hath redeemed Jerusalem.
The Lord hath made bare his holy arm in the eyes of all the nations;
And all the ends of the earth have seen the salvation of our God.
Depart ye, depart ye, go ye out from thence, touch no unclean thing;
Go ye out of the midst of her; be ye clean, ye that bear the vessels of the Lord.
For ye shall not go out in haste, neither shall ye go by flight
For the Lord will go before you; and the God of Israel will be your rearward.

SEVENTY-EIGHTH LESSON.

ISA. 55. Ho, every one that thirsteth,
Come ye to the waters, and he that hath no money;
Come ye, buy, and eat;
Yea, come, buy wine and milk without money and without price.
Wherefore do ye spend money for that which is not bread?
And your labor for that which satisfieth not?
Hearken diligently unto me, and eat ye that which is good,
And let your soul delight itself in fatness.
Incline your ear, and come unto me; hear, and your soul shall live:
And I will make an everlasting covenant with you, even the sure mercies of David.
Behold, I have given him for a witness to the peoples
A leader and commander to the peoples.

Behold, thou shalt call a nation that thou knowest not,
  And a nation that knew not thee shall run unto thee,
Because of the Lord thy God, and for the Holy One of Israel;
  For he hath glorified thee.
Seek ye the Lord while he may be found,
  Call ye upon him while he is near:
Let the wicked forsake his way, and the unrighteous man his thoughts:
  And let him return unto the Lord, and he will have mercy upon him; and to our
    God, for he will abundantly pardon.
For my thoughts are not your thoughts,
  Neither are your ways my ways, saith the Lord.
For as the heavens are higher than the earth, so are my ways higher than
    your ways,
  And my thoughts than your thoughts.
For as the rain cometh down and the snow from heaven
  And returneth not thither, but watereth the earth,
And maketh it bring forth and bud, and giveth seed to the sower and bread to
    the eater;
  So shall my word be that goeth forth out of my mouth:
It shall not return unto me void, but it shall accomplish that which I please,
  And it shall prosper in the thing whereto I sent it.
For ye shall go out with joy,
  And be led forth with peace:
The mountains and the hills shall break forth before you into singing,
  And all the trees of the field shall clap their hands.
Instead of the thorn shall come up the fir tree,
  And instead of the brier shall come up the myrtle tree:
And it shall be to the Lord for a name,
  For an everlasting sign that shall not be cut off.

ISA. 66.   REJOICE ye with Jerusalem, and be glad for her, all ye that love her:
  Rejoice with joy for her, all ye that mourn over her:
That ye may suck and be satisfied with the breasts of her consolations;
  That ye may milk out, and be delighted with the abundance of her glory.

For thus saith the Lord, Behold, I will extend peace to her like a river, and
the glory of the nations like an overflowing stream,
*And ye shall suck thereof; ye shall be borne upon the side, and shall be dandled
upon the knees.*

As one whom his mother comforteth, so will I comfort you;
And ye shall be comforted in Jerusalem.

And ye shall see *it*, and your heart shall rejoice,
And your bones shall flourish like the tender grass.

SEVENTY-NINTH LESSON.

LUKE I. My soul doth magnify the Lord,
And my spirit hath rejoiced in God my Saviour.

For he hath looked upon the low estate of his handmaiden:
For behold, from henceforth all generations shall call me blessed.

For he that is mighty hath done to me great things;
And holy is his name.

And his mercy is unto generations and generations
On them that fear him.

He hath shewed strength with his arm;
He hath scattered the proud in the imagination of their heart.

He hath put down princes from *their* thrones,
And hath exalted them of low degree.

The hungry he hath filled with good things;
And the rich he hath sent empty away.

He hath holpen Israel his servant, that he might remember mercy
(As he spake unto our fathers) toward Abraham and his seed for ever.

Blessed *be* the Lord, the God of Israel;
For he hath visited and wrought redemption for his people.

And hath raised up a horn of salvation for us in the house of his servant
David
As he spake by the mouth of his holy prophets which have been of old.

Salvation from our enemies, and from the hand of all that hate us;
To shew mercy towards our fathers, and to remember his holy covenant;

The oath which he sware unto Abraham our father,
 To grant unto us that we being delivered out of the hand of our enemies
Should serve him without fear,
 In holiness and righteousness before him all our days.
Yea and thou, child, shalt be called the prophet of the Most High :
 For thou shalt go before the face of the Lord to make ready his ways;
To give knowledge of salvation unto his people in the remission of their sins,
 Because of the tender mercy of our God, whereby the dayspring from on high shall visit us,
To shine upon them that sit in darkness and the shadow of death ;
 To guide our feet into the way of peace.

LUKE 2. And she brought forth her firstborn son ; and she wrapped him in swaddling clothes, and laid him in a manger,
 Because there was no room for them in the inn.
And there were shepherds in the same country abiding in the field, and keeping watch by night over their flock.
 And an angel of the Lord stood by them, and the glory of the Lord shone round about them: and they were sore afraid.
And the angel said unto them, Be not afraid ; for behold, I bring you good tidings of great joy which shall be to all the people :
 For there is born to you this day in the city of David a Saviour, which is Christ the Lord.
And this *is* the sign unto you ; Ye shall find a babe wrapped in swaddling clothes, and lying in a manger.
 And suddenly there was with the angel a multitude of the heavenly host praising God, and saying,
Glory to God in the highest,
 And on earth peace among men in whom he is well pleased.

EIGHTIETH LESSON.

SELECTED PASSAGES.

AND the Word became flesh, and dwelt among us, and we beheld his glory,
Glory as of the only-begotten from the Father, full of grace and truth.

For in him dwelleth all the fullness of the Godhead bodily.
Faithful is the saying, and worthy of all acceptation, that Christ Jesus came into the world to save sinners.

Come unto me, all ye that labor and are heavy laden,
And I will give you rest.

Take my yoke upon you, and learn of me;
For I am meek and lowly in heart:

And ye shall find rest unto your souls.
For my yoke is easy, and my burden is light.

For God so loved the world, that he gave his only begotten Son,
That whosoever believeth on him should not perish, but have eternal life.

For God sent not the Son into the world to judge the world;
But that the world should be saved through him.

For when we were yet weak,
In due time Christ died for the ungodly.

For scarcely for a righteous man will one die; yet peradventure for the good man some one would even dare to die.
But God commendeth his own love toward us, in that while we were yet sinners, Christ died for us.

For there is one God, one mediator also between God and men,
Himself man, Christ Jesus, who gave himself a ransom for all.

Since then the children are sharers in flesh and blood,
He also himself in like manner partook of the same;

That through death he might bring to nought him that had the power of death, that is, the devil;
And might deliver all them who through fear of death were all their lifetime subject to bondage.

For verily not to angels doth he give help,
But he giveth help to the seed of Abraham.

Wherefore it behoved him in all things to be made like unto his brethren,
That he might become a merciful and faithful high priest in things pertaining to God,

To make propitiation for the sins of the people.
> *For in that he himself hath suffered being tempted, he is able to succor them that are tempted.*

Wherefore also God highly exalted him,
> *And gave unto him the name which is above every name:*

That in the name of Jesus every knee should bow, of *things* in heaven and *things* on earth and *things* under the earth,
> *And that every tongue should confess that Jesus Christ is Lord, to the glory of God the Father.*

I therefore, the prisoner in the Lord, beseech you to walk worthily of the calling wherewith ye were called,
> *With all lowliness and meekness,*

With long-suffering, forbearing one another in love;
> *Giving diligence to keep the unity of the Spirit in the bond of peace.*

There is one body, and one Spirit,
> *Even as also ye were called in one hope of your calling:*

One Lord, one faith, one baptism, one God and Father of all, who is over all, and through all, and in all.
> *But unto each one of us was the grace given according to the measure of the gift of Christ.*

Wherefore he saith, When he ascended on high, he led captivity captive,
> *And gave gifts unto men.*

But ye are come unto mount Zion, and unto the city of the living God, the heavenly Jerusalem,
> *And to innumerable hosts of angels, to the general assembly and church of the firstborn who are enrolled in heaven,*

And to God the judge of all, and to the spirits of just men made perfect, and to Jesus the mediator of a new covenant,
> *And to the blood of sprinkling that speaketh better than that of Abel.*

For our citizenship is in heaven;
> *From whence also we wait for a Saviour, the Lord Jesus Christ:*

Who shall fashion anew the body of our humiliation, *that it may be* conformed to the body of his glory,
> *According to the working whereby he is able even to subject all things unto himself.*

So then ye are no more strangers and sojourners,
> *But ye are fellow-citizens with the saints, and of the household of God,*

Being built upon the foundation of the apostles and the prophets,
 Christ Jesus himself being the chief corner stone:
In whom each several building, fitly framed together, groweth into a holy temple in the Lord;
 In whom ye also are builded together for a habitation of God in the Spirit.
Now unto the King eternal, immortal, invisible, the only wise God, be honor and glory for ever and ever.
 Amen.

EIGHTY-FIRST LESSON.

SELECTED PASSAGES.

The hour cometh, and now is, when the true worshippers shall worship the Father in spirit and truth:
 For such doth the Father seek to be his worshippers.
God is a Spirit:
 And they that worship him must worship in spirit and truth.
No man hath beheld God at any time:
 If we love one another, God abideth in us, and his love is perfected in us:
Hereby know we that we abide in him, and he in us,
 Because he hath given us of his Spirit.
And he that keepeth his commandments abideth in him, and he in him.
 And hereby we know that he abideth in us, by the Spirit which he gave us.
If ye then, being evil, know how to give good gifts unto your children,
 How much more shall your heavenly Father give the Holy Spirit to them that ask him?
For John indeed baptized with water;
 But ye shall be baptized with the Holy Ghost not many days hence.
They therefore, when they were come together, asked him, saying,
 Lord, dost thou at this time restore the kingdom to Israel?
And he said unto them, It is not for you to know times or seasons, which the Father hath set within his own authority.
 But ye shall receive power, when the Holy Ghost is come upon you.
Jesus answered, Verily, verily, I say unto thee,
 Except a man be born of water and the Spirit, he cannot enter into the kingdom of God.

That which is born of the flesh is flesh;
  And that which is born of the Spirit is spirit.
Marvel not that I said unto thee, Ye must be born anew.
  The wind bloweth where it listeth, and thou hearest the sound thereof,
But knowest not whence it cometh, and whither it goeth:
  So is every one that is born of the Spirit.
But ye are not in the flesh, but in the Spirit, if so be that the Spirit of God dwelleth in you.
  But if any man hath not the Spirit of Christ, he is none of his.
And if Christ is in you, the body is dead because of sin;
  But the Spirit is life because of righteousness.
But if the Spirit of him that raised up Jesus from the dead dwelleth in you,
  He that raised up Christ Jesus from the dead shall quicken also your mortal bodies through his Spirit that dwelleth in you.
So then, brethren, we are debtors, not to the flesh, to live after the flesh:
  For if ye live after the flesh, ye must die:
But if by the Spirit ye put to death the deeds of the body, ye shall live.
  For as many as are led by the Spirit of God, these are sons of God.
For ye received not the spirit of bondage again unto fear;
  But ye received the spirit of adoption, whereby we cry, Abba, Father.
The Spirit himself beareth witness with our spirit,
  That we are children of God:
And if children, then heirs; heirs of God, and joint-heirs with Christ;
  If so be that we suffer with him, that we may be also glorified with him.
It is expedient for you that I go away: for if I go not away, the Comforter will not come unto you;
  But if I go, I will send him unto you.
And he, when he is come, will convict the world in respect of sin, and of righteousness, and of judgment:
  Of sin, because they believe not on me;
Of righteousness, because I go to the Father, and ye behold me no more;
  Of judgment, because the prince of this world hath been judged.
I have yet many things to say unto you, but ye cannot bear them now.
  Howbeit when he, the Spirit of truth, is come, he shall guide you into all the truth:
For he shall not speak from himself; but what things soever he shall hear, *these* shall he speak:
  And he shall declare unto you the things that are to come.

THE MESSIAH AND HIS KINGDOM.

He shall glorify me:
For he shall take of mine, and shall declare it unto you.

All things whatsoever the Father hath are mine:
Therefore said I, that he taketh of mine, and shall declare it unto you.

If ye love me, ye will keep my commandments.
And I will pray the Father, and he shall give you another Comforter, that he may be with you for ever, even the Spirit of truth:

Whom the world cannot receive; for it beholdeth him not, neither knoweth him: ye know him;
For he abideth with you, and shall be in you.

Things which eye saw not, and ear heard not, and *which* entered not into the heart of man,
Whatsoever things God prepared for them that love him.

But unto us God revealed *them* through the Spirit:
For the Spirit searcheth all things, yea, the deep things of God.

Know ye not that ye are a temple of God,
And that the Spirit of God dwelleth in you?

If any man destroyeth the temple of God, him shall God destroy;
For the temple of God is holy, which temple ye are.

But the fruit of the Spirit is love, joy, peace, longsuffering, kindness, goodness, faithfulness, meekness, temperance:
Against such there is no law.

And they that are of Christ Jesus have crucified the flesh with the passions and the lusts thereof.
If we live by the Spirit, by the Spirit let us also walk.

Likewise the Spirit also helpeth our infirmity, for we know not how to pray as we ought:
But the Spirit himself maketh intercession for us with groanings which cannot be uttered.

And he that searcheth the hearts knoweth what is the mind of the Spirit;
Because he maketh intercession for the saints according to the will of God.

The grace of the Lord Jesus Christ, and the love of God, and the communion of the Holy Ghost, be with you all.
Amen.

EIGHTY-SECOND LESSON.

REV. 4-5. AFTER these things I saw, and behold, a door opened in heaven, and the first voice which I heard, *a voice* as of a trumpet speaking with me, one saying,
Come up hither, and I will shew thee the things which must come to pass hereafter.
Straightway I was in the Spirit:
And behold, there was a throne set in heaven, and one sitting upon the throne;
And he that sat *was* to look upon like a jasper stone and a sardius:
And there was a rainbow round about the throne, like an emerald to look upon.
And round about the throne *were* four and twenty thrones:
And upon the thrones I saw four and twenty elders sitting, arrayed in white garments; and on their heads crowns of gold.
And out of the throne proceed lightnings and voices and thunders.
And there were seven lamps of fire burning before the throne, which are the seven Spirits of God;
And before the throne, as it were a glassy sea like unto crystal:
And in the midst of the throne, and round about the throne, four living creatures full of eyes before and behind.
And they have no rest day and night, saying,
Holy, holy, holy, is the Lord God, the Almighty, which was and which is and which is to come.
And when the living creatures shall give glory and honor and thanks to him that sitteth on the throne,
To him that liveth for ever and ever,
The four and twenty elders shall fall down before him that sitteth on the throne,
And shall worship him that liveth for ever and ever, and shall cast their crowns before the throne, saying,
Worthy art thou, our Lord and God, to receive the glory and the honor and the power:
For thou didst create all things, and because of thy will they were, and were created.
And I saw in the midst of the throne and of the four living creatures, and in the midst of the elders, a Lamb standing, as though it had been slain,
Having seven horns, and seven eyes, which are the seven Spirits of God, sent forth into all the earth.

And he came, and he taketh *the book* out of the right hand of him that sat on the throne. And when he had taken the book, the four living creatures and the four and twenty elders fell down before the Lamb,
Having each one a harp, and golden bowls full of incense, which are the prayers of the saints.

And they sing a new song, saying, Worthy art thou to take the book, and to open the seals thereof:
For thou wast slain, and didst purchase unto God with thy blood men of every tribe, and tongue, and people, and nation,

And madest them *to be* unto our God a kingdom and priests;
And they reign upon the earth.

And I saw, and I heard a voice of many angels round about the throne and the living creatures and the elders;
And the number of them was ten thousand times ten thousand, and thousands of thousands;

Saying with a great voice, Worthy is the Lamb that hath been slain
To receive the power, and riches, and wisdom, and might, and honor, and glory, and blessing.

And every created thing which is in the heaven, and on the earth, and under the earth, and on the sea, and all things that are in them, heard I saying,
Unto him that sitteth on the throne, and unto the Lamb, be the blessing, and the honor, and the glory, and the dominion, for ever and ever.

And the four living creatures said, Amen.
And the elders fell down and worshipped.

EIGHTY-THIRD LESSON.

REV. 14. AND I saw, and behold, the Lamb standing on the mount Zion,
And with him a hundred and forty and four thousand, having his name, and the name of his Father, written on their foreheads.

And I heard a voice from heaven, as the voice of many waters, and as the voice of a great thunder:
And the voice which I heard was as the voice of harpers harping with their harps:

And they sing as it were a new song before the throne, and before the four living creatures and the elders:
And no man could learn the song save the hundred and forty and four thousand, even they that had been purchased out of the earth.
They *are* they which follow the Lamb whithersoever he goeth.
These were purchased from among men, to be the firstfruits unto God and unto the Lamb.
And in their mouth was found no lie:
They are without blemish.
And I saw another angel flying in mid heaven, having eternal good tidings to proclaim unto them that dwell on the earth,
And unto every nation and tribe and tongue and people;
And he saith with a great voice, Fear God, and give him glory; for the hour of his judgment is come:
And worship him that made the heaven and the earth and the sea and fountains of waters.
And I heard a voice from heaven saying, Write, Blessed are the dead which died in the Lord from henceforth:
Yea, saith the Spirit, that they may rest from their labors; for their works follow with them.
After these things I heard as it were a great voice of a great multitude in heaven, saying, Hallelujah;
Salvation, and glory, and power, belong to our God: for true and righteous are his judgments;
For he hath judged the great harlot, which did corrupt the earth with her fornication,
And he hath avenged the blood of his servants at her hand.

REV. 19. And a second time they say, Hallelujah.
And her smoke goeth up for ever and ever.
And the four and twenty elders and the four living creatures fell down
And worshipped God that sitteth on the throne, saying, Amen; Hallelujah.
And a voice came forth from the throne, saying, Give praise to our God,
All ye his servants, ye that fear him, the small and the great.
And I heard as it were the voice of a great multitude, and as the voice of many waters, and as the voice of mighty thunders, saying, Hallelujah:
For the Lord our God, the Almighty, reigneth.

Let us rejoice and be exceeding glad, and let us give the glory unto him:
For the marriage of the Lamb is come, and his wife hath made herself ready.

And it was given unto her that she should array herself in fine linen, bright and pure:
For the fine linen is the righteous acts of the saints.

And he saith unto me, Write,
Blessed are they which are bidden to the marriage supper of the Lamb.

And I saw an angel coming down out of heaven, having the key of the abyss and a great chain in his hand.
And he laid hold on the dragon, the old serpent, which is the Devil and Satan, and bound him for a thousand years, and cast him into the abyss, and shut it, and sealed it over him,

That he should deceive the nations no more, until the thousand years should be finished:
After this he must be loosed for a little time.

And I saw thrones, and they sat upon them, and judgment was given unto them:
And I saw the souls of them that had been beheaded for the testimony of Jesus, and for the word of God,

And such as worshipped not the beast, neither his image, and received not the mark upon their forehead and upon their hand; and they lived and reigned with Christ a thousand years.
This is the first resurrection.

Blessed and holy is he that hath part in the first resurrection: over these the second death hath no power;
But they shall be priests of God and of Christ, and shall reign with him a thousand years.

EIGHTY-FOURTH LESSON.

REV. 21. AND I saw a new heaven and a new earth;
For the first heaven and the first earth are passed away; and the sea is no more.

And I saw the holy city, new Jerusalem, coming down out of heaven from God,
Made ready as a bride adorned for her husband.

And I heard a great voice out of the throne saying, Behold, the tabernacle of God is with men, and he shall dwell with them,
And they shall be his peoples, and God himself shall be with them, and be their God:

And he shall wipe away every tear from their eyes;
And death shall be no more; neither shall there be mourning, nor crying, nor pain, any more: the first things are passed away.

And he carried me away in the Spirit to a mountain great and high,
And shewed me the holy city Jerusalem, coming down out of heaven from God, having the glory of God:

Her light was like unto a stone most precious, as it were a jasper stone, clear as crystal:
Having a wall great and high;

Having twelve gates, and at the gates twelve angels;
And names written thereon, which are the names of the twelve tribes of the children of Israel.

And the twelve gates were twelve pearls; each one of the several gates was of one pearl:
And the street of the city was pure gold, as it were transparent glass.

And I saw no temple therein:
For the Lord God the Almighty, and the Lamb, are the temple thereof.

And the city hath no need of the sun, neither of the moon, to shine upon it:
For the glory of God did lighten it, and the lamp thereof is the Lamb.

And the nations shall walk amidst the light thereof:
And the kings of the earth do bring their glory into it.

And the gates thereof shall in no wise be shut by day (for there shall be no night there):
And they shall bring the glory and the honor of the nations into it:

And there shall in no wise enter into it any thing unclean, or he that maketh an abomination and a lie:
But only they which are written in the Lamb's book of life.

REV. 22. And he shewed me a river of water of life, bright as crystal,
Proceeding out of the throne of God and of the Lamb, in the midst of the street thereof.

And on this side of the river and on that was the tree of life, bearing twelve *manner of* fruits, yielding its fruit every month:
And the leaves of the tree were for the healing of the nations.

And there shall be no curse any more:
And the throne of God and of the Lamb shall be therein:

And his servants shall do him service;
And they shall see his face; and his name shall be on their foreheads.

And there shall be night no more; and they need no light of lamp, neither of the sun;
For the Lord God giveth them light: and they shall reign for ever and ever.

Blessed are they that wash their robes, that they may have the right *to come* to the tree of life,
And may enter in by the gates into the city.

I Jesus have sent mine angel to testify unto you these things for the churches.
I am the root and the offspring of David, the bright, the morning star.

And the Spirit and the bride say, Come.
And he that heareth, let him say, Come.

And he that is athirst, let him come:
He that will, let him take the water of life freely.

He which testifieth these things saith, Yea: I come quickly.
Amen: come, Lord Jesus.

The grace of the Lord Jesus be with the saints.
Amen.

INDEX OF SELECTIONS.

DEUT.	PAGE.
28	19
32	87

JOB.	PAGE.
7	63
14	64
33	18
36	44
37	45
38	46

PSALMS.	PAGE.
1	1
2	109
3	75
4	86
6	16
7	90
8	34
9	98
13	71

	PAGE.
15	1
16	110
17	71
18	43
19	48
20	70
21	111
22	112
23	52
24	31
25	12
26	89
27	72
28	69
29	49
30	67
32	16
33	37
34	56
36	14
37	83
39	62

	PAGE.
40	17
41	79
42	9
43	9
44	79
45	114
46	77
47	31
48	4
49	92
50	95
51	10
53	94
54	91
56	82
57	89
61	73
62	68
63	5
65	53
66	7
67	119

PAGE.	PAGE.	PAGE.
68......115	117......29	40......123
71...... 74	118......29	42......121
72......118	119......99	51......127
73...... 81	119......101	52......128
76......110	121......54	53......125
80...... 14	122...... 7	55......128
81...... 82	123......91	60......123
82...... 93	124......70	61......126
84...... 6	125......54	66......129
85...... 13	127......55	
86...... 76	130......11	**HOSEA.**
87...... 8	131...... 2	PAGE.
88...... 85	132...... 3	14...... 20
89...... 33	134...... 8	
90...... 63	135......32	**JOEL.**
91...... 52	138......23	PAGE.
92...... 22	139......41	2...... 21
93...... 34	142......80	
94...... 93	143......80	**HABAKKUK.**
95...... 5	144......59	PAGE.
96...... 34	146......55	3...... 95
97...... 36	147......60	
98......115	148......27	**ZECHARIAH.**
99...... 36	149......28	PAGE.
100...... 6	150......29	13......26
101...... 2		
102...... 66	**PROVERBS.**	**MATT.**
103...... 24	PAGE.	PAGE.
104...... 39	3......102	11 : 28–30......132
107...... 50	4......103	
108...... 25	8......105	**LUKE.**
110......109	14......107	PAGE.
111...... 38		1 : 46–55......130
112...... 2	**ISAIAH.**	1 : 68–79......131
113...... 26	PAGE.	2 : 7–14......131
115...... 78	9......121	11 : 13......134
116...... 26	11......119	
	12......122	**JOHN.**
	35......120	PAGE.
		1 : 14......132
		3 : 5– 8......134
		3 : 16, 17......132

INDEX OF SELECTIONS.

	PAGE.
4 : 23, 24	134
14 : 15–17	136
16 : 7–15	135

ACTS.
	PAGE.
1 : 5– 8	134

ROMANS.
	PAGE.
5 : 6– 8	132
8 : 9–18	135
8 : 26, 27	136

I. COR.
	PAGE.
2 : 9, 10	136
3 : 16, 17	136

II. COR.
	PAGE.
13 : 14	136

GAL.
	PAGE.
5 : 22–25	136

EPH.
	PAGE.
2 : 19–22	133
4 : 1– 8	133

PHIL.
	PAGE.
2 : 9–11	133
3 : 20, 21	133

COL.
	PAGE.
2 : 9	132

I. TIM.
	PAGE.
1 : 16	132
1 : 17	134
2 : 5	132

HEB.
	PAGE.
2 : 14–18	132
12 : 22–24	133

I. JOHN.
	PAGE.
3 : 23	134
4 : 12, 13	134

REV.
	PAGE.
4	137
5	138
14	138
19	139
20	140
21	141
22	142

www.ingramcontent.com/pod-product-compliance
Lightning Source LLC
Chambersburg PA
CBHW030346170426
43202CB00010B/1260